Understanding Multicultural Education

Equity for All Students

Understanding Multicultural Education

Equity for All Students

Francisco Rios
University of Wyoming

Christine Rogers Stanton
Montana State University

ROWMAN & LITTLEFIELD EDUCATION

A division of

ROWMAN & LITTLEFIELD PUBLISHERS, INC.
Lanham • New York • Toronto • Plymouth, UK

Published by Rowman & Littlefield Education
A division of Rowman & Littlefield Publishers, Inc.
A wholly owned subsidary of The Rowman & Littlefield Publishing Group, Inc.
4501 Forbes Boulevard, Suite 200, Lanham, Maryland 20706
http://www.rowmaneducation.com

Estover Road, Plymouth PL6 7PY, United Kingdom

British Library Cataloguing in Publication Information Available

Library of Congress Cataloging-in-Publication Data

Rios, Francisco, 1956–
  Understanding multicultural education : equity for all students / Francisco Rios and
Christine Rogers Stanton.
     p. cm.
  Includes bibliographical references.
  ISBN 978-1-60709-861-4 (cloth : alk. paper) — ISBN 978-1-60709-862-1 (pbk. : alk.
paper) — ISBN 978-1-60709-863-8 (electronic)
  1. Multicultural education—United States. 2. Educational equalization—United States.
I. Stanton, Christine Rogers, 1975- II. Title.
  LC1099.3.R56 2011
  370.1170973—dc22   2011005260

♾ ™ The paper used in this publication meets the minimum requirements of American
National Standard for Information Sciences—Permanence of Paper for Printed Library
Materials, ANSI/NISO Z39.48-1992.

Printed in the United States of America

Contents

Foreword

Valerie Ooka Pang, San Diego State University

How can we, as a nation, ensure that each student is well educated? Rios and Stanton have written a passionate and informative book about multicultural education, a field dedicated to educational equity for our democracy. They have taken their extensive experience with mainstream and nondominant culture populations and created an insightful foundational text. The authors believe multicultural education can play a critical role in improving the education of all students. Rios and Stanton's writing style is easily accessible and is an excellent resource for school district board members, parents, teachers, and others who want to understand the goals and underlying principles of multicultural education.

As the authors wisely explain, multicultural education is a journey and not a destination. Therefore, Rios and Stanton include discussion of the history of the field, which assists in setting the context for the field. Multicultural education arose out of our nation's struggle for civil rights from the early twentieth century through today. They carefully describe how multicultural education is an important component of our democracy, a democracy that is built upon our culturally and linguistically diverse society.

Throughout the text, the authors encourage their readers to reflect upon the knowledge being taught in schools. For example, they carefully point out how critical race theory challenges the use of knowledge of the dominant population as the main dogma that is taught in schools. However, schools in a nation dedicated to social justice must include the funds of knowledge that students from nondominant culture communities bring to schools; social, family, and cultural capital, information about their family histories, knowledge from their communities, and networking resources should also be embraced in the curriculum of our democratic nation. Not only is the knowledge from diverse students part of our nation, but their social and cultural capital can be used to create culturally responsive and relevant instruction. This will result in more effective education. These and other practices are described in the book. For example, policy makers and educators will benefit from summary charts that provide important sources of exemplary practices, culturally diverse role models, cultural values, and assessment avenues.

Most importantly, Rios and Stanton discuss the work of Paulo Freire, the Brazilian educator, who believed that oppressed people must become active participants working to address social injustice. Through education, they can become empowered to make changes in society, changes based on the preservation of civil and human rights. Rios and Stanton describe schools that have adopted the Freirian philosophy; one of these schools is the Native American Community Academy in New Mexico. Not only is culturally relevant knowledge being taught, such as language coursework in Navajo, Lakota, and Spanish, but also students participate in service learning projects where leadership and college preparation skills are taught to ensure that the next generation of young people are being prepared to become responsible, purposeful citizens.

Rios and Stanton's text, *Understanding Multicultural Education: Equity for All Students*, challenges their readers to consider the type of schools and society that we want to build and sustain in our nation. Using the metaphor of a house, the authors identify critical elements that form multicultural education, from myths about the field to addressing social oppression. In order for education to be equitable, school board members, educators, and parents must consider how schools can enhance their commitment to providing educational equity.

Acknowledgments

Many people have helped us on our own journeys as multicultural educators. We wish to thank the leaders in the field of critical multicultural education who have provided guidance for our own learning and thinking, including James Banks, Carl Grant, Christine Sleeter, Gloria Ladson-Billings, Sonia Nieto, Linda Tuhiwai Smith, and many others. In addition to the guidance provided by these individuals, we also thank the various organizations that have inspired our work, including the National Association for Multicultural Education and the Social Justice Research Center at the University of Wyoming.

Our colleagues at the University of Wyoming and Montana State University have provided tremendous support and shared passion for our work. Several individuals, including Nancy Gallavan at the University of Central Arkansas and Shelley Zion, CRUE Center at the University of Colorado—Denver, provided extensive feedback for this specific work. We thank Valerie Ooka Pang for her forward to this work.

We also thank the Rowman & Littlefield Publishing Group for believing in the value of this work but also the importance of works aimed at fostering educational equity. We thank in particular Editor Tom Koerner for agreeing to publish this work and for his valued recommendations. We also thank Lindsey Schauer and Mirna Araklian for their assistance in moving this work to production. We also thank Kelly Applegate for moving the work into print.

Our families, friends, and mentors have influenced and inspired us in the journey leading to this work. Francisco wishes to thank his family for making the house he returns to a home. In particular, he thanks his partner for life, Debra, and his two children Zekial and Natalia, the light in his eyes.

Christine thanks her mentors at the University of Wyoming and the University of Iowa, who have shown her the way. She is forever grateful to, and inspired by, the unconditional support and love of her family members, friends, and husband, Brad.

Most importantly, we thank those who have taught us patiently, and without judgment, about multicultural education—parents, grandparents, and community members—and our greatest teachers of all; our students.

Preface

The importance of pursuing an education that has both a multicultural and social justice-oriented focus is as great as ever. Our nation seems more divided about questions of difference and diversity, about equity and justice, than even before the election of Barack Obama in 2008. American public education is under attack, including questions about its broadest purposes (democratic participation), the qualifications of the educators, and the quality of education.

Yet we continue to maintain profound hope when considering the women and men who infuse their work in schools with creativity, purposefulness, and dedication. In particular, we are guided by those educational professionals who infuse their work with an understanding of the power education can have when students' social identities are considered and affirmed. We also recognize the power of education when students learn about other forms of diversity. And we are especially impressed when educators are able to engage the students in their charge with activities and actions aimed to transform unequal social conditions.

The purpose of this book is to make the goals, ideas, theories, principles, and practices of multicultural education accessible to the widest possible audience of educational professionals and stakeholders. Multicultural education as an academic discipline has evolved over the last 25 years to become a promising, productive, and positive approach to education within an increasingly diverse schooling context. Without a more complete understanding of the ideals of multicultural education, misconceptions persist that undermine its legitimate implementation.

The net result is either a superficial implementation of the principles of multicultural education or no implementation at all. At the end, it is our hope that educational professionals move beyond the heroes and holidays approaches to diversity in education and recognize that it is a philosophy of inclusion, equity, and democracy.

* * *

Throughout this book, we emphasize the importance of approaching multicultural education as a journey, not a destination. The writing of this book was a journey made possible by our own experiences as students, teachers, scholars, and teacher educators. Therefore, we introduce ourselves and our reasons for writing this book by sharing parts of our journeys.

Francisco

I came to appreciate the importance of multicultural education as a student, growing up during the height of the Chicano (Mexican-American) political movement of the late 1960s and early 1970s, in the Denver Public Schools. I had experiences not uncommon to many nondominant culture students. These included being tracked into vocational professions, experiencing a curriculum void of anything about my culture, and recognizing that the only language of value was English. This was despite the fact that the schools that I attended were dominated by the presence of Chicano students.

During my high school years, Chicano students from throughout the Southwest were participating in walkouts, called *blowouts*, to protest inferior educational experiences in their schools. Community leaders and activists within the Chicano community in Denver began to organize these walkouts there as well.

The first issue we wanted to address was the lack of Chicano teachers. When asked, the administration said that there were no Chicano teachers to be found. So the first blowouts were centered on demanding that Chicano teachers be found and hired. While the administration at first balked, seeing nearly 90% of their students walking out of school led them to find and hire a Chicano teacher within a fairly short amount of time.

"It worked," we thought and realized.

So the next blowouts were to demand that Chicano Studies be taught. We wanted to learn more about the history and contemporary experiences of the Chicano community. Once again, the administration balked and we walked out. And, again, within a short period of time, the administration had scheduled several sections of Chicano Studies for the coming semester.

At one point the lunchroom had been newly repainted. Along with a fresh coat of paint, a big hamburger and hotdog were painted on one side of a wall. We decided to walk out asking that some artwork depicting the Chicano experience appear on the lunchroom wall. Within a short time, a Chicano muralist was hired to paint a mural near the lunchroom entrance.

These walkouts were important for several reasons. First, students felt empowered to make their concerns known. Second, structural changes to the school were the result of these walkouts. Third, and perhaps most importantly, as students walked out, we gathered to listen to political speeches detailing the oppression of our communities (and others, including what was occurring in the African American and American Indian communities) but also stories of resistance. It was in these moments that I began to develop a critical cultural consciousness.

At the same time that this was occurring, one summer I was employed as a tutor for *La Academia del Barrio*. The program was for students from kindergarten to sixth grade. The program was directed by Chicano leaders, all the teachers were Chicanos, and the curriculum was taught completely from a Chicano perspective: Mayan math to teach computation principles, Chicano history for social studies, and even *ballet folklorico* for physical education.

I began to see the possibilities of an education that reflected the culture and cultural values of my home community. Later, I would recognize the importance of learning about the African American and American Indian experiences. These came about as a student teacher in an urban Milwaukee school and a student teaching experience on the Cheyenne River Indian Reservation in South Dakota.

As I became a teacher, I worked diligently to provide space for students to learn about their own cultural backgrounds, but also to teach them to understand the experiences of communities different from their own.

Christine

I came to learn about multicultural education as a teacher. Growing up in rural Nebraska and later in a midsized Wyoming town, I was surrounded by people who looked like me, talked like me, and—I assumed—thought like me. I also assumed that young people everywhere had similar (i.e., ambivalent) views regarding cultural diversity.

It wasn't until college in the Midwest that I began to question this perspective. After study abroad in South America, coursework in Latin American and African literature, and work with young people from urban and migrant backgrounds, I realized I wanted to become a teacher. To an extent, I felt cheated in terms of my own educational past, and teaching became a way to learn.

During my third year of teaching in a town bordering a Native American reservation, I taught a remedial English course for juniors. The course was called "Foundations of English 11" and was supposedly a slimmed-down version of the "regular" course, which surveyed American literature.

One day, three-fourths of the way through the first semester, we were tackling a popular work of the Western literary canon. I can't remember which one, and I don't know that it matters. I most likely asked a question like, "What do you think the theme of this short story is?" While the question was probably worded in a way to encourage student participation, I undoubtedly had a specific answer in mind.

Finally, one of my Native students reached his maximum threshold for frustration. He slammed his textbook closed and growled, "Why do we have to do this? We're in the dummy class." I fumbled for a moment that was, hopefully, imperceptible to my students, and responded with something along the lines of, "This isn't the dummy class—you guys are completely capable of doing the same work as the other classes."

A few weeks later, the students were preparing to give speeches. The student who'd grown so frustrated worked relentlessly to craft his speech. I didn't think much about it until the day of the actual speech, when he strode purposefully to the front of the classroom holding the hardcopy of his speech delicately in his hands. He stood behind the podium, and proceeded to deliver an eloquent, flawless speech that he had memorized completely.

That experience, like many others, taught me much about multicultural education. As a teacher, instructional coach, and teacher educator, I began to connect the many experiences, which centered on one key concept: hearing the story-experiences of my students and their communities.

* * *

Our unique journeys have intertwined with those of many other people—mentors, scholars, teachers, parents, grandparents, and, most importantly, students. It is important to realize that the path to multicultural education is not only a journey, but that it is a journey shared by many people. It is not one of isolation or inexperience. Instead, we hope you will look to others, as we have, for guidance in finding your way.

Chapter 1

Introduction

Our very different journeys have led us to this house of multicultural education. Throughout this book, we discuss key topics related to multicultural education through the metaphor of a house. Like a physical house, the house of multicultural education consists of walls (which can both perpetuate and resist oppression), the living room (a place for practical conversations), the kitchen (where myths are cooked up and assumptions made), the rooftop (promises for future growth in the field), and the tool shed (resources for implementation).

In addition, the house itself is situated within a community and neighborhood, which also influences the way we view and feel about the physical place. Various roads lead through the community to the house, and the path we choose influences the nature of our individual journeys to the house of multicultural education.

While multicultural education fits the metaphor of a physical house well, it is far more than a structure. Too often, educators and other people involved with and invested in improving educational opportunities (the people we refer to as "educational stakeholders") encounter a basic structure of multicultural education: implementation of isolated practices or adopting a curriculum that claims to address needs of diverse students without fully interrogating these choices. As a result, multicultural education may be implemented superficially or incompletely.

A house can be a physical shelter, but it can also be much more than that: It can be a home. To make multicultural education our home, we need to commit wholly to it. Like other homes, multicultural education must be a place where everyone feels welcome and safe, a place to gather both in times of happiness and when we need support. It must influence every part of our professional and personal lives, and it must be the place to which we return for renewal.

This book is about embarking on a journey to the house of multicultural education with the hope that you will feel comfortable not only with opening the door to responsive education, but with making it your home. Throughout the book, we describe the basic structures that define a house, as we share specific ideas for practice in schools. We also introduce you to the theory and scholarship that can guide your passion as responsive educators and educational stakeholders. This passion is the key to opening the door to a new, more socially just home.

* * *

This book provides an introduction to a relatively new and growing academic discipline known as multicultural education. Multicultural education has activist roots, emerging from the Civil Rights Movement, and it is aimed at assuring educational equity for student populations all too often underserved and marginalized in schools. It has grown to include a variety of conceptual understandings, school and classroom-based recommended practices, national organizations with annual conferences, and professional journals. Multicultural education has impacted the experiences students have in schools, the teaching approaches and curriculum teachers have employed, and the academic articles and books that scholars have produced.

But multicultural education has also had to face its critics and its critiques, further evidence of the vibrancy of the discipline. Given its deeply political activist roots, and the fact that almost all people have strong emotional reactions (positive, mixed, and negative) about the implications of an increasingly diverse U.S. society, it would surprise us if there were not some people who disagree with the major concepts that have emerged from the discipline. While most acknowledge that academic achievement in schools in the United States falls unacceptably low for some groups of students, especially those based on race, class, and gender, what must be done to close the achievement gap is hotly debated.

To be sure, much of the disagreement and critique is a result of misunderstanding the central aims and ideals of multicultural education. Therefore, the goal of this chapter is to introduce you to the central ideals of multicultural education. We describe how the principles of multicultural education emerge from and extend central tenets of education in a democracy.

Following the overview of ideals, a brief history of the field as an academic discipline is provided. Finally, this chapter discusses the analogy of a house as an organizing device for the rest of the book to guide you through various rooms within the multicultural education field. Our intent is to provide you a blueprint of the house of multicultural education. We also ask you to keep in mind that, like any blueprint, this book only provides a general overview. The specific details, often as important, are beyond the scope of this introductory book.

CENTRAL TENETS OF MULTICULTURAL EDUCATION

Like any academic discipline, a series of tenets or accepted truths guide the work within the field. Often these tenets are assumed but never explicitly stated. We begin with the truths that we believe guide the field of multicultural education so that you can more fully understand this academic discipline. We discuss these tenets below in no particular order of importance.

First, multicultural scholars believe that there can be no excellence in education until and unless there is equity in academic outcomes. In 1979, Ron Edmonds asked the question: Are there any effective schools in the United States for nondominant culture students? The question rested on the belief that schools *can* be structured to assure the success of all students. Thus began a new focus on effective schools.

Unfortunately, many educators who followed up on this work did not focus on the equity dimension of this question, instead using some other general measures of effectiveness or excellence. To be true to the original intent would require that people ask: Are schools effective for all social groups of students by gender, by race, by class, etc.? Without a positive answer to the equity question, there cannot be a positive answer to the excellence question. In short, multicultural educators are keenly interested in academic excellence AND equity.

A second tenet of multicultural education is that this nation's diversity is an asset and a valuable resource that can serve to spur both equity and excellence. While this makes common sense, the United States has a long history of seeing diversity as a problem. For example, it was common to describe nondominant culture students as being culturally deficient since their cultural norms—values, beliefs, and behaviors—differed from mainstream, White, middle-class norms.

This deficiency orientation has persisted and continues to find its way into much of the educational discourse. Consider, for example, how the work of Ruby Payne (2001) around the "culture of poverty" has been welcomed into school districts nation wide. The critiques of this work rest largely on the fact that it employs a deficiency orientation.[1]

Multicultural educators have argued that diversity is not a problem but rather serves as an important asset that can be used in service of helping schools reach the excellence to which they aspire. The opportunity to hear multiple viewpoints and experiences, to learn with and from people different from oneself, and to gain a wider appreciation for the possibilities of how to think and live are just part of the value of diversity that strengthens the nation.

A third tenet is that multicultural education is for everyone. A common assumption people often hold when considering whether, when, and where to employ multicultural education is that it needs to be implemented when classrooms and schools have significant student diversity. This is certainly true.

But it is equally argued that classrooms and schools that lack student diversity are in special need of multicultural education to assure that their students are prepared for the diversity in communities they will encounter across the nation. In those schools lacking student diversity, it requires more purposeful attention to assuring that multicultural education is brought into the classroom via the curriculum, instructional activities, and community connections. This idea can be extended to assert that it is not who the teachers and students are in a particular school but what they do that makes an education multicultural.

A related tenet is that both the educational professional and her/his students' identities matter when it comes to teaching and learning. We recognize that people (administrators, school staff, teachers, students, and volunteers) bring all that they are—culturally, linguistically, psychologically, socially, etc.—to the schools where they learn and work. These identities, whether they are affirmed or dismissed, are central to how people come to understand and respond to their experiences in schools. To disregard these identities is to disregard a person's very essence, that which gives meaning to one's life. As Adrienne Rich (1986) described it:

> When those who have the power to name and to socially construct reality choose not to see you or hear you . . . when someone with the authority of a teacher . . . describes the world and you are not in it, there is a moment of psychic disequilibrium, as if you looked in the mirror and saw nothing. (p. 166)

Importantly, multicultural educators also understand that identities are changing and developing (i.e., fluid and dynamic). They also understand that those within the same identity group do not all share the same worldview. Consider the difference within the Mexican American experience, for example, based on differences in gender, class, regional affiliation, immigration status, generation, Spanish language ability, and so forth. As in this example, multicultural educators also assert that people do not have one identity but rather have many identities. Some of these identities are more important than others, often depending upon time and place (that is, context). They recognize that teachers and students also can make choices about which identities to emphasize, depending upon the context.

The last tenet is a belief that multicultural education can play a vital role in improving the educational experience for all students. That is not only a belief but also a hope that multicultural educators bring to their work. What becomes important to understand is that there are many ways people have approached multicultural education, as should be the case. After all, it would be hypocritical to say that there is only one way to approach the issue of diversity in education. We detail differing approaches to multicultural education in Chapter 3.

However, we assert that some approaches to multicultural education are more effective than others; that is, some have taken an approach to multicultural education that is not consistent with the field at all (for example, having "taco day" and then believing that multicultural education efforts have been completed). Additionally, we understand that multicultural education is constantly evolving just as educators must constantly evolve. Another way responsive educators think about this is that multicultural education is a path and not a place. What we do know is that multicultural education will not happen naturally. It must be understood and then deliberately pursued.

Postulates of Multicultural Education

Another way to investigate the tenets of multicultural education is to look at the central postulates or major claims evidenced in multicultural education research. Fortunately, Christine Bennett (2001) has completed a review of this research, working to uncover the postulates or major claims about multicultural education. Bennett asserts that this review of the research demonstrates four postulates with several subclaims embedded within each.

The first postulate is related to the idea of *curriculum reform*. Multicultural educators recognize that knowledge is socially constructed. That is, people create knowledge; these people have their own prejudices, biases, and limitations. Multicultural educators also acknowledge that people with different points of view, who have grown up and learned in different social and cultural settings, create different knowledge. That means that these knowledge bases, different as a result of being created by different people, are sometimes in conflict.

Within this conflict, however, multicultural educators also recognize that some people's knowledge is more valued (and believed) than others. The

African proverb explains it best: "Until the lion has his or her own story-teller, the hunter will always have the best part of the story." That is, some group's knowledge is deemed superior (usually the social group with the most power). The result is that students usually learn only one perspective in a school's curriculum—usually that of the social group in power.

As an example of the social construction of knowledge, consider that at the end of the War of Independence from Britain, the newly created U.S. government sponsored a variety of initiatives designed to create a uniquely American identity, ideology, mythology, and even language. Noah Webster, for example, worked to create an American English dictionary of words distinct from the British language. At the same time, British textbooks were banned.

Bennett asserts that one postulate evidenced in multicultural education research is that the decision to privilege a Eurocentric perspective in the curriculum in the United States is a tool of cultural imperialism intended to devalue the experiences and perspectives of nondominant culture people while simultaneously maintaining and preserving existing (and unequal) power relations.

A second set of postulates focus on *equity pedagogy*. Multicultural educators believe that all children have special talents and the capacity to learn. In addition, these educators assert that these students bring cultural assets (that is, assets that are developed and prized in the cultural communities from which they come) and use these assets to promote and facilitate learning. The major goal of education, then, is to make it possible for all children to reach their fullest potential. Multicultural educators believe that schools can and must be organized to assure that students have every opportunity to maximize their talents and capacities.

An important part of this equity pedagogy is recognition that teachers' and students' cultural backgrounds and sense of ethnic identity influence teaching and learning, as we stated earlier. But it also includes enriching the curriculum with a variety of perspectives and using instructional strategies that complement and extend student learning.

A third set of postulates revolves around the development of *multicultural competence*. This postulate or claim suggests that the reduction of prejudice is not only possible but is also desirable. Prejudice reduction is a difficult task that must be engaged in purposefully and deliberately. Multicultural educators believe that schools, as public spaces where young people are required to spend a significant part of their day, may be the best place to accomplish this task.

Another claim related to multicultural competence is that individuals can become multicultural without rejecting their familial worldview and identity to function comfortably in other cultural milieus or contexts. That is, the development of multicultural competence allows individuals to hold on to their own cultural identities while coming to live, learn, and work in a variety of different cultural settings.

The final postulate described in the research is related to *societal equity*. Given that the field of multicultural education owes much of its development to the Civil Rights Movement, it focuses on broader social issues as well as those that surface in schools. Most multicultural educators recognize that broader social change is necessary to bring about comprehensive equity in education (that is, access, participation, and achievement in schools). Unemployment, underemployment, homelessness, racism/sexism/homophobia, environmental degradation, and segregation in housing all play their own role in undermining educational excellence and equity. Therefore, many multicultural educators believe that their work must include activities aimed at promoting positive social change.

Related to this, multicultural educators recognize that social change is both possible and consistent with basic democratic values and the American creed. Consider that the greatest advances made in the United States were related to social change efforts—the abolition of slavery during the Civil War, women's right to vote in the early 1900s, the integration of schools and housing during the Civil Rights Movement, the provisions for individuals with disabilities, and the current dialogue about language diversity and sexual orientation are but a few examples.

MULTICULTURAL EDUCATION AS A DEMOCRATIC PROJECT

As suggested in Bennett's (2001) last postulate, the work in multicultural education is consistent with democratic principles and creed. At one level, much of multicultural education is centered upon empowering students to become active participants in our nation's democracy. Schools have a significant role to play in this important goal given that people are not born with the knowledge of what it means to live and learn in a democracy. However, an important tension revolves around how we become united given the diversity of the people of the United States. Multicultural educators believe that this nation's diversity strengthens our democracy.

Walter Parker (2003) has addressed this question of the role of diversity in democracy. Parker asserts that there are three parts of an advanced or strong democracy wherein diversity is a central concept: participatory democracy, creative democracy, and multicultural democracy.

Participatory Democracy. Many people think that participating on voting day, honoring the freedom to speak, worshiping in the religion of their choice, allowing for individuality, and assuring equality before the law are the essence of democracy. Participatory democracy asks us go deeper and become more fully engaged in dialogue and action to foster alternative ways of living that eliminate poverty, violence, hopelessness, and family disruption—not out of altruism but out of civic attitude. Parker argues that as long as families and communities are in peril, our democracy is in peril.

Creative Democracy. Creative democracy asserts that democracy is not yet finished. The United States began on the path of democracy with the forging of the Constitution. The nation's democracy was advanced considerably with the abolition of slavery, the enfranchisement of women's right to vote, and the gains made during the Civil Rights Movement. Still, our democracy has a way to go toward the ideals enshrined in this nation's founding documents: the Constitution, the Declaration of Independence, and the Bill of Rights.

It is also true that the democratic ideal is constantly changing as our society changes. Consider how democracy is being re/considered after the events on September 11, 2001. The question becomes how do we move from stating our ideal to helping people achieve it? This is a hopeful perspective in that young people come to learn that they have an active role to play in the movement down the path toward the democratic ideal. Parker argues that democracy is a way of life, a way of being.

Multicultural Democracy. Multicultural democracy asks of participatory democracy: who is participating, who is not, and on whose terms? It asks of creative democracy, how wide can we make the path? Multicultural democracy challenges the idea of eliminating or ignoring or tolerating diversity while simultaneously challenging cultural assimilation. Rather, Parker asserts that unity arises from our diversity, is a result of our diversity, and therefore considers diversity as a democratic virtue. Consider diversity, then, an enemy of totalitarianism since it affirms different worldviews, values systems, and political perspectives. This is the essence of what democracy is about and gives it its vitality.

A recent work that has added considerably to this discussion comes from the University of Washington's Center for Multicultural Education and is titled *"Democracy and Diversity: Principles and Concepts for Educating Citizens in a Global Age."*[2] It asserts:

> Multicultural societies are faced with the challenge of creating nation-states that recognize and incorporate the diversity of their citizens *and* embrace an overarching set of shared values, ideals, and goals to which all citizens are committed. Only when a nation-state is unified around a set of democratic values such as human rights, justice, and equality can it secure the liberties of cultural, ethnic, language, and religious groups and enable them to experience freedom,

justice, and peace. Citizens who understand this unity-diversity tension and act accordingly do not materialize from thin air; they are educated for it. (p. 7)

A BRIEF HISTORY OF MULTICULTURAL EDUCATION

In order to more fully understand the field of multicultural education, it is helpful to understand its historical roots. James Banks, considered by many one founder of multicultural education, has provided a historical overview, which we draw upon for this brief summary. Banks (2004) identified five different eras of multicultural education, of which the civil rights era has been the most foundational. During each era, ideas about diversity were further defined and concepts more fully developed.

The earliest foundations of multicultural education can be found in the works of scholars in the early 1900s who attempted to both foster a positive sense of ethnic identity for their social group and to acknowledge those efforts at social change engaged in by nondominant culture communities. This work included championing the positive experiences and knowledge of specific ethnic communities as part of legitimate academic knowledge. Consider the work of W. E. B. Du Bois and Carter G. Woodson in detailing the histories of African American communities and the work of Carlos Boulson of the Filipino community.

During the 1940s and 1950s, there emerged strong scholarly work around intergroup relations. This era was led by scholars who were interested in understanding how and why people develop racist and prejudicial postures. As important, these scholars were interested in understanding how to begin to change these attitudes and perceptions, which serve as justification for racist and sexist actions, as well as how to foster the broader development of more democratic dispositions. Gordon Allport's classic work *The Nature of Prejudice* (1954/1979) is an example of the scholarly work being done during this era.

This era also focused on the negative impact that biased attitudes and actions had on nondominant culture people. Kenneth and Mamie Clark, for example, were psychologists who documented the negative impact of segregation on the identities and self-esteem of African American children. Their testimony in desegregation court cases was pivotal in court decisions to promote integration. An important limitation of the work in this era is that the focus was on the development of prejudice in individuals and not on the ways schools and other institutions create policies and practices—such as tracking or school segregation—that promote those prejudices and allow discrimination to occur.

The third era, the ethnic studies movement, occurred during the 1960s and was marked by the development of alternative histories and perspectives about specific ethnic communities. It focused on the issues these communities experienced in terms of discrimination and, as important, the ways these communities pushed against that oppression. The works of Rudy Acuña and Vine Deloria, Jr. serve as two examples of scholars documenting both the oppression and resistance that their communities (Chicano and Native American, respectively) experienced.

The 1970s saw the rise of the fourth era, which Banks has called the modern ethnic studies movement. This era was marked by attention to the ways institutions, such as schools, are structured to promote academic inequality. As a result, the era was also characterized by efforts in infuse knowledge generated by ethnic studies scholars throughout the entire school curricula. A related emphasis was the preparation of teachers, primarily in colleges of education, to more responsively address the needs of nondominant culture students.

Importantly, during this era, attention began to expand beyond ethnicity as the sole area of concern to greater attention to gender, sexual orientation, socioeconomic class, and disability concerns. It also began to draw attention to how these social identities interacted, such as gender with ethnicity or race with disability. It was during this time that multicultural education as a distinct academic field, different from ethnic studies, came into existence.

Banks identifies the current era as the critical multiculturalism era. At this time, the complexity of the discipline of multicultural education has become much more evident as well as its changing and expanding nature. But the field has also seen the ways public and private institutions have taken key concepts from the academic discipline and misused and misapplied them for their own ends. For example, business people have used the affirmation of diversity for marketing purposes and most public institutions have included a commitment to diversity in their mission statements without making any meaningful policy changes. Even well-meaning teachers have used multicultural education to pursue a superficial attention to diversity in curriculum and instruction, via tokenism in the curriculum or via an assimilationist ideology, while moving away from the social change nature of the field that served as its foundation.

As a result, critical multiculturalism has emerged to re-center the field back to its critical and activist foundations, bringing with it greater attention to issues of power and privilege as well as the importance of institutional and social change. In short, even within the field of multicultural education, it is important to investigate what people mean when they say they implement an education that is multicultural.

A WORD ABOUT WORDING

One of the challenges associated with writing a book is that written language has multiple meanings depending upon who is using the words and their broad purposes. Language, therefore, can be potentially problematic. As we wrote the book we had to make decisions about wording, punctuation, and other grammatical practices. For example, we used quotation marks within this text when referring to phrases or sentence-level statements made by others and we include the citations for those quotes. In addition, we have highlighted the irony behind some contestable terms by, on occasion, also using quotation marks.

However, we struggled with words such as "minority," since the word may be inaccurate and inappropriate in some, if not many, cases. We considered terms like "students of color" but then realized it narrowed diversity to skin color differences exclusively. So we settled on "nondominant culture" students. While a little awkward, it represents the fact that these students are not part of the dominant cultural group.

In addition, we utilized terms commonly used in today's schools, such as "best practices," even though these concepts may not reflect our professional or personal views of what constitutes "best practices" when considering the complexity of education as a whole and multicultural education specifically. The usage of such terms, and the resulting positioning of some groups to determine what constitutes best practices, should be questioned carefully.

Another term that can be potentially troubling is the term "cultural competence." Many multicultural educators use this term and, when explaining their work, we use this since that is the language they use. But the idea of cultural competence suggests a set of skills and abilities that can be attained as if reaching some end point. We see the skills and abilities to affirm diversity, in all its forms, as continually evolving and dependent upon the group with whom you are working. Scholars and advocates in the field are using the term "cultural responsiveness" in an attempt to underscore the contextual nature of a person's cultural abilities.

We recognize the deeply political nature of our language choices. Such was especially evident in our decision to limit the use of the word "citizen," replacing it with words like "participants" or "people." The reason for this was our recognition that there are millions of people living in the United States who are not "citizens" but who nonetheless are productive contributors to this nation. In addition, federal courts have determined that these students have a right to a free and public education, despite their citizenship status.[3] We urge you to consider the political nature of the language used not only in this text but also in school settings where you might find yourself.

We also want to provide these definitions of terms so that they might be helpful to you as you read the rest of the book.

Definition of Terms

In offering the following terms here we recognize that others might define them differently. However, we use these terms in this book in the following way.[4]

- Prejudice—A set of rigid and unfavorable attitudes toward a particular group or groups that is formed in disregard of facts. It is an unsupported judgment usually accompanied by disapproval.
- Stereotype—A preconceived or oversimplified generalization often involving negative beliefs about a particular group. Negative stereotypes are frequently at the base of prejudice. The danger of stereotyping is that it no longer considers people as individuals but rather categorizes them as members of a group who all think and behave similarly.
- Discrimination—Unequal *treatment* based on unfair categorization. When you act on your prejudices, you engage in discrimination. Discrimination often involves keeping people out of activities or places because of the social group to which they belong.
- Sexism—Assigning certain characteristics to people on the basis of their gender, with an assumption of superiority or inferiority, and resulting in unequal treatment.
- Racism—Combines the false assumption that race determines psychological and cultural traits with the belief that one race is superior to another. Based on the belief that certain groups are inferior, racists justify discriminating against these groups. The term racism is being used here in a broad sense to include discrimination against both ethnic and racial peoples. It also requires power to make the racism have its greatest impact.
- Passive Racism—Beliefs and actions that contribute to maintenance of racism without advocating oppression. The conscious or unconscious maintenance of beliefs and behaviors that support the system of racism and racial domination.
- Active Racism—Actions that have as their stated goal the maintenance or perpetuation of the system of racism and oppression. Includes advocating for the continued subjugation of members of the targeted group and protection of the rights of members of the agent group. Active racism is often supported by an underlying ideology of superiority over the Other.
- Homophobia—Literally, the fear of homosexuality. Prejudicial hatred of homosexuality, which often results in discriminatory practices and sometimes even violent attacks.

- Ethnocentrism—The tendency to judge other groups by the norms, values, behaviors, and expectations of your own group; that is, your own group is at the center of all other groups. Ethnocentrism includes the tendency to elevate the value of your group.
- Scapegoating—The deliberate act of blaming an individual or group for things they did not really do. Prejudicial attitudes and discriminatory acts lead to scapegoating. Members of the disliked group are denied social privileges such as housing and employment. They are usually politically powerless to defend themselves.
- Institutional Racism—Discrimination that is not individual in nature but is embedded in the policies and practices of particular institutions like schools, banks, governments, and so on. That is, the institution carries out its tasks in ways that allow some people to gain privileges while others are denied access to those privileges. The decision to have higher interest rates for home loans in low-income neighborhoods is an example of institutional racism against poorer persons. There is usually no intent to discriminate on the part of those who work in the institution, but the results of their implementation of policies and practices are nonetheless discriminatory and maintain status differences among groups of people.

We hope that you will raise questions about various terms used in education and even those included in this book. Developing a critical mind is one of the most important steps in the journey to multicultural education. We hope that you will think critically about the language being used both within this book and within the national dialogue about diversity and difference.

Book Overview

The chapters that follow will provide a more detailed description of multicultural education as an academic discipline. To accomplish this, we will use a house as an organizing device and as a metaphor for the discipline. We borrow this notion of a house as a metaphor from Alicia Gaspar de Alba's (1997) book *Chicano Art: Inside-Outside the Master's House*. A house is an apt metaphor to use since it allows us to see how different areas within the field, like different rooms within a house, are connected together by a common structure.

In real life, people's homes are different. As in the field of multicultural education, then, people might describe the field differently given the distinct vantage point that they take. And this difference is valued given that seeking multiple perspectives is a hallmark of the field. As authors, then, we are describing multicultural education from the house that we inhabit and the particular vantage point from which we view it.

In short, a more careful look into the field of multicultural education will find that while the basic structure of the field can be described, there are important differences in how other people conceive of the academic discipline (for example, what postulates around multicultural education they would include and not include). As important, as you read this book keep in mind that the multicultural education house is still not completely constructed. As we have stated, the academic discipline is constantly growing and changing.

In Chapter 2, we provide a description of the location of the house. That is, we provide a broader lens to look at the city, town, reservation, community, neighborhood, or barrio where this multicultural education house is located. Through this metaphor, then, we provide a broader lens on the field of multicultural education. We look at the main issues that multicultural education attempts to address. This chapter also details the broader field of education looking at current policies, many embedded in public law such as the No Child Left Behind Act legislation, which we characterize as in conflict with efforts to make an education multicultural. Yet we also see positive signs in the community, and in the field of education broadly, that give us hope.

Chapter 3 provides a description of the streets where the house is located. Correspondingly, we begin by looking at the many paths that multicultural education has taken by way of the different theoretical orientations that have been advanced within the field. After sharing what we believe are the key goals of multicultural education that all orientations share, we detail four distinct theoretical stances most prominent within the field. Again, we see these multiple paths as strength. We end this chapter by describing a metaphorical fork in the road that we see within the field. On one path are efforts that continue to limit multicultural education to superficial changes in curriculum and instruction with very little meaning. The other path leads to a resurgence of the critical, social activist elements within the field that served as its earlier foundation as described above.

As one approaches any house, the first thing visible of the structure are the walls. In Chapter 4, we too look at the walls of multicultural education for ways in which they have been weathered as well as the ways in which they have been reconditioned. More specifically, this chapter will look at the various forms of oppression that have battered nondominant culture communities as well as other marginalized social groups and the forms and levels these oppressions have taken. This will include both a description of the various forms of oppression (racism, sexism, classism, etc.) and an overview of how privilege plays a central role in the maintenance of this oppression. But these communities are constantly revitalized by the resistance that is displayed against the oppression. Oppression and resistance are the walls of a house that is multicultural.

Chapter 5 provides us a glimpse of the living room, the common place where people—family, friends, neighbors, and strangers—gather together to meet and talk everyday. For multicultural education, this room provides us an opportunity to share the everyday practices of education as they might be, given the principles of multicultural education. This includes the common areas of education: curriculum (what is taught), instruction (how it is taught), assessment (how it is measured), and classroom organization and management (how teaching and learning are organized). This chapter also focuses on relations schools have with administrators and school district personnel, as well as on the ways schools invite or do not invite parents and community members into our house.

In the kitchen, we often have our most engaged conversations over a cup of coffee or a tamale plate. The kitchen is also the place where things get cooked up. In Chapter 6, then, we turn our attention to the things that are being cooked up about multicultural education. This chapter provides a description of the common myths and misconceptions of multicultural education. We provide our most engaged response to these myths and misconceptions in ways that help illuminate both the complexity of the field and some of the underlying tensions evident within the discipline.

In the early evening, the family might go up to the rooftop to enjoy a cool evening breeze and watch the moon and stars. In this same way, we provide a description of the promising practices in the field of multicultural education and future directions in Chapter 7. Some of the most promising practices include those that recognize the assets that students (and their parents and community members) bring to the teaching-learning experience as a means to replace the traditional approach, which focused on their deficiencies. This chapter includes a glimpse at important work being done to engage youth in action research projects, to recognize race as a more central concept in education, to understand the ways communities and parents contribute to students' educational success, and to link democracy and multicultural education more fully.

We end, in Chapter 8, in the tool shed. Like the tools we find to help keep the house in working order, to recondition it, and to expand it, in the multicultural education tool shed we find those things that help the profession to be sustained and to grow. These include the books, journals, professional organizations, and Web sites that serve the field of multicultural education. While we will not provide a major inventory of all these tools, we do highlight the most important of these as we have identified them in the tool shed that sits outside of our house of multicultural education.

* * *

We hope, dear reader, that this work provides you with a broad enough of an overview of the field of multicultural education to allow you to think more fully about it: from its roots and its foundations, to its everyday implementation and its future directions. We hope it helps you to think about how to talk about the field more accurately and to participate in the dialogue about its role in schooling. And we hope that this book provides you with a reason to be committed to acting in ways that promote an education that is multicultural.

NOTES

1. See, for example, Gorksi, 2008a.
2. Banks, McGee Banks, Cortés, Hahn, Merryfield, Moodley, Murphy-Shigematsu, Osler, Park, & Parker, 2005.
3. Plyer v Doe, 457, U.S. 202 (1982).
4. Adapted from Hardiman & Jackson, 1997.

Chapter 2

The Town

The Broader Context of Multicultural Education

Have you ever wondered *why* schools are structured as they are? For example, in many elementary schools one teacher is placed with a group of about 25 students for a whole school year. The teacher's curriculum is often guided by themes, commonly corresponding with the seasons of the year. These classrooms are walled off and teachers often work in isolation.

In most junior high schools, the structure of schools suddenly shifts from having one teacher to having seven or eight teachers who may have 150 students on any one day. These junior high school students may change teachers at the midpoint of the school year. The curriculum is sectioned off and driven by academic disciplines such as math, science, music, English/language arts, and social studies.

And what about high schools? They often physically look and are run like factories and, like the junior high schools, operate on a clearly defined time schedule marked by bells indicating the beginning and ending of a class period. Once again, the content is broken down into specific academic topics much like what occurs in junior high school. And for all three levels, schools start in early fall and end in late spring. But why?

So where did these ideas about how to enact schooling come from? Why were schools structured in these ways? High schools were influenced by the industrial revolution and were structured much like factories. They were, in effect, preparation for industries most in need of workers at the turn of the century. Organizers of high schools wanted students to respond to the bells and whistles of these factories and to be obedient when given directions. They also wanted to section off academic subjects in the same way that tasks in the factory are compartmentalized.

In addition, the comprehensive high school allowed increased economic efficiency on several levels, since it allowed hundreds of students to gather in one building, utilized the expertise of a small number of faculty members, and adhered to curriculum that focused on development of basic skills. Junior high schools were, then, just preparation for the high school.

As this discussion attests, the broader societal purposes at a particular moment often dictate how schools get structured, frequently ignoring what might be best for the student. These societal purposes are often determined by the ruling class with little, if any, regard for the complex needs of students, families, and communities.

In recent years, many junior high schools have been transformed into middle schools. Much of this transformation was based on new understandings of early adolescence, which recognized the tremendous developmental changes these 11–15 year-olds experience. A change of name from junior high to middle school was supposed to represent a change in the way schooling was done for early adolescents.

Middle schools serve as a bridge between elementary school and high school by assigning teams of three to five teachers to work with the same students over the course of the year. Like in elementary schools, the teachers worked to coordinate their curriculum around themes while still being clear about the academic disciplines. Finally, students are placed in groups, sometimes called pods or villages, so that they operate as small schools within the larger school.

We share these examples because we encourage readers to ask such broad question such as *what* is the purpose of schooling? If the answer is to promote an informed, democratic society, then we would want to ask *how* might schools be structured for such? Then we would ask what role might multicultural education play in achieving these educational aims.

In this chapter, we focus on the broadest possible settings in which multicultural education finds itself. Just as a house is located in a city or town, so multicultural education is part of the broader context of education and schooling. The city or town is not just a matter of where the house is located but profoundly influences what takes place there and what can occur.

Just as schools were structured for certain social, economic, and political purposes, it is important to understand the contemporary social, economic, and political conditions impacting multicultural education. Some of these work to support the implementation of multicultural education while others serve to undermine these efforts, both of which we describe in this chapter. We end this chapter with a short description of where the field is headed and what scholarly advances in other areas are helping the academic discipline to grow and move forward.

PRIMARY REASONS FOR PURSUING
MULTICULTURAL EDUCATION

We begin by describing the reasons most often cited for pursuing multicultural education. While we describe these as different reasons, they sometimes overlap and often people will call forth more than one of these reasons for advancing an education that is multicultural.

Addressing the Demographic Imperative

To begin, many people describe how the demographics around cultural and linguistic diversity in the United States have changed in the past decades and that schools are approaching a majority of students from non-White backgrounds.[1] White students in 2007–08 made up only 54% of the student population while Latina/o students represented 22%, African American students were 17%, Asian/Pacific Islander students 5%, and American Indian students were 1% of the national student population. Forty percent of all students come from low-income families; 12% of all students have some form of disability. The number of students who spoke a language other than English at home was 11 million, representing 21% of the entire student population.[2] Five percent of the student population is classified as English Language Learners.

In addition, multicultural educators often note how this change in the student demographics is not mirrored in the teaching profession. Consider that while Whites make up just barely half of the entire student population, in 2007–08 they represented 83% of the teaching workforce.[3] Added to this is the fact that these teachers often lack substantial and positive interactions with people different from themselves and often lack the desire to teach in school environments marked by high levels of diversity.

For many, this creates a cultural mismatch between teachers and the students in their charge. Teachers often know very little about who their students are in terms of their social identity, how they live and learn, and how to make meaningful connections to them within the classroom environment. In short, multicultural education is seen as a demographic imperative.

Closing the Achievement Gap

These demographic descriptions by themselves mean very little. However, a second reason often cited for the need for multicultural education is the historical and contemporary low academic achievement performance of students from certain social groups based on race, class, and gender on nearly all measures.[4]

Consider the National Assessment of Educational Progress (NAEP) exam, a national exam of math and reading proficiency.[5] In 2008–2009, for example, 83% of White students scored "basic" or better in reading in the 8th grade. Correspondingly, 59% of Latina/os and 56% of African Americans scored basic or better in reading. In 8th grade math, 82% of Whites scored basic or above, yet only 56% of Latina/os and 49% of African American students scored basic or above. These percentages of students scoring basic or better *decrease* as students move from 4th grade to 8th grade. In terms of graduation from high school,[6] of people over 25, 92% of Whites, 84% of African Americans, and 62% of Latina/os have garnered their high school degree.

Education Week[7] (August 18, 2010) reported that while more Latina/o and African American students are taking the ACT, a standardized assessment used by universities and colleges to determine admissions, they also continue to score lower than their White counterparts. Specifically, only 4% of African Americans and 11% of Latina/os met the levels ACT has defined as indicating college readiness. This is in comparison to 30% of White test takers. With respect to graduation from college, these numbers decline from 33% for Whites, to 19% for African Americans, and 13% for Latina/os.

Importantly, these statistics have real economic consequences in terms of employment and financial security. The U.S. Department of Labor[8] shows that students who have not attained a high school diploma have an unemployment rate of 15% and an average weekly salary of $454. By comparison, those with a high school degree have an unemployment rate of 10% and earn $626 weekly. Those who graduate with a bachelor's degree from college have a 5% unemployment rate and earn on average $1,025 weekly. Over the course of a year, then, those who don't complete high school are three times as likely to be unemployed and earn nearly $30,000 less a year when compared to their peers who have earned a bachelors degree.

Such data influence educational decisions regularly, especially in light of requirements in No Child Left Behind legislation and the Individuals with Disabilities Education Act to disaggregate student achievement by subgroup to assure that no subgroup is failing in schools. If the achievement gap persists in a school, funding or other resources may be compromised.

When addressing the achievement gap, school leaders may seek to support nondominant culture students within the structure of the traditional school, without substantially altering the way teaching occurs for mainstream students. For example, Latina/o students may be targeted for extra testing to determine English proficiency. Students who do not attain a set level of proficiency may be provided special services, such as enrollment in support classes or specialized test preparation programs.

In another common response, teachers may participate in professional development aimed at modifying instruction to meet diverse learning styles of nondominant culture students in the general classroom setting. For example, instead of utilizing lecture-based instruction, teachers may learn to incorporate cooperative learning activities into their teaching. In this example, teachers may modify their teaching slightly to better meet the needs of students, but much of the curriculum, assessment, and management approaches may not change significantly.

In the two above examples, nondominant culture students are viewed as possessing deficiencies or differences, and schooling remains relatively unchanged for the majority of students. The status quo of schooling, what Sleeter and Grant (2009) call the "business as usual" model (see Chapter 3), is unchallenged under such approaches. As a result, education does not evolve or improve dramatically for nondominant culture—or mainstream—students.

In other cases, schools and/or individual teachers may choose to substantially alter the educational structure as a means to boost achievement of nondominant culture students. For example, they may modify their curriculum to focus upon historical accounts that directly challenge the textbooks, they may work to connect students to the community through service learning, or they may offer programs that cultivate cultural and academic growth, such as bilingual academies.

Reversing the Failure of Assimilation

A third reason for pursuing multicultural education is the assertion that the gaps in academic performance are tied to past efforts to eradicate students' social and cultural identities. Much of educational policy historically has been directed at assimilating nondominant culture students into the dominant culture (i.e., White, middle class). In essence, the attempt was to make these students culturally, socially, and linguistically White. And it does so by "subtracting" students' cultural and linguistic backgrounds[9] and heritages or via a process Joel Spring (2009) describes as "deculturalization."

Some of the most blatant examples of these come from Native American boarding school experiences, though Latina/os, African Americans, and immigrants have had similar experiences. The idea of removing Native American students from their home and local community and into boarding schools was the beginning of efforts aimed at erasing students' cultural and linguistic backgrounds. Once in these boarding schools, these students' traditional clothing was burned, their Indian names were changed, their hair was cut, and they were forbidden to speak any language other than English. The education they received avoided any discussion of their rich heritage, their experiences with oppression, or the ways in which their people resisted that oppression.[10] The goal of cultural assimilation as described by Carlisle Boarding School founder, Richard H. Pratt (1892/1973), was to "kill the Indian in him, and save the man."

The result was that many of these students felt ostracized from their home community as a result of these assimilationist schooling experiences. And while many of these students resisted their assimilation in significant ways, others of these students in many instances did embrace their new "American" identities. For this latter group, discrimination in employment and housing and interpersonal relations left them feeling as if they had given up everything about who they were for no gain. That is, society asked of these students to become American but they were still not accepted in mainstream communities, workplaces, or in social settings.

In retrospect, most educators would now acknowledge the immoral assertion that someone should give up his/her home culture and language in order to become academically successful. Unfortunately, this assimilationist ideology still persists today. In short, despite efforts at cultural assimilation, the academic achievement gap persists and remains.

Unlike assimilative efforts, which strive to eliminate differences, multicultural education affirms cultural identities and recognizes the importance of diversity.[11] Responsive teachers view diversity not as a melting pot, but as an orchestra. While each instrument in an orchestra is unique and wonderful in its own right, its contribution to the larger whole is significant. In this analogy, individuals maintain their specific cultural and personal traits, yet these unique attributes enhance the overall quality of the society—the orchestra—as a whole. Responsive educators utilize equity-based pedagogy to demonstrate respect for diversity in their classrooms.

Fostering Cross-Cultural Responsiveness

It is not uncommon for some to suggest that, due to internationalization and globalization, our world is shrinking. We see and hear about natural disasters, political upheaval, or economic collapse as they are happening or soon afterward. We can get on a plane and be in a completely different cultural surround in a matter of hours. We can communicate via e-mail, video conferencing, or telephone with people who live in nearly every part of the globe. The products we purchase, the fine arts we enjoy (such as music, art, film), and the ideas we learn, both in school and out, can come as much from beyond our own borders as from within them.

Multicultural education advocates recognize the global nature of our world. But they also recognize that internationalization and globalization have also increased and enhanced the diversity within our own border. As a result, these advocates believe that all students need to be prepared to cross a variety of cultural and linguistic borders, to operate effectively in these diverse settings, and to feel comfortable doing so. For these advocates, multicultural education is about developing the cultural responsiveness associated with living in a globalizing society.[12]

Cultural responsiveness is an ability to move across a variety of different cultural contexts and to do so both effectively and comfortably. In multicultural education, much of this effort also includes helping teachers to become culturally competent. Culturally competent teachers, according to Jerry Diller and Jean Moule (2005), exhibit "the ability to successfully teach students who come from cultures other than your own. It entails mastering complex awareness and sensitivities, various bodies of knowledge, and a set of skills that, taken together, underlie effective cross-cultural teaching" (p. 2).

Two general approaches to the development of cross-cultural competence seem to dominate.[13] One approach is to describe the stages of cross-cultural competence, seeing these as developmental (that is, the first stage sets a person up for the second stage, which sets a person up for the third stage, etc.). These models, such as those described by Diller and Moule (2005), typically have four clusters of stages. The first is self-awareness. The second is an awareness of one's feelings and thoughts about difference and diversity generally. The third stage is knowledge and awareness of other cultural groups. The final stages are usually described as cross-cultural skill development with a list of general skills one can employ to work effectively with those who are different.

Some of these stage models suggest that the development of cross-cultural competence is linear, that is, that one must develop fully in one stage before they can move to the next. Other models suggest that cross-cultural stages are concurrent, that is, a person can work on developing all of these stages at the same time. Importantly, these stage models recognize that developing cross-cultural competence is a life-long journey since you can never fully know yourself, your own cultural groups, and all the possible cultural groups that a person may come in contact with.

A second approach, and evident in this last stage, is the identification of general cross-cultural competency skills. Generally these include knowledge, attitudes, and skills in the areas of self-awareness, awareness of difference, awareness of the impact of racism and prejudice (historically and contemporarily), learning about cultural patterns, and, finally, skills related to using cultural knowledge for professional purposes. For the latter, in the case of teaching, it includes understanding students' culturally influenced learning styles and communication styles, adapting the curriculum to reflect the diversity of students in the classroom, and using a variety of participation and assessment strategies that are culturally relevant.[14]

What should also be evident in these cross-cultural competence approaches is that it is absolutely essential to address issues of power, racism, and privilege if cross-cultural competence is to be developed. A note of caution about these stages and lists is that they are often written from the perspective of preparing White, middle-class people for the cross-cultural experiences they are sure to experience. Unfortunately, we most often see this aim in elite, suburban schools where students are prepared for international business and political opportunities, often without also asking these students to uncover and challenge the ways in which these opportunities may represent a new version of colonialism. Likewise, these students are often not taught the ways in which oppression occurs within the United States.

Teachers and other stakeholders may approach the goal of enhanced cultural responsiveness in different ways and on many different levels of action. While the most common approach is to focus on commonalities and increase communication skills, some teachers, administrators, community members, and policy makers endeavor to explicitly and systematically address the discriminatory practices that are embedded in the institution and society. As such, a goal closely related to increasing cultural responsiveness is the effort to reverse educational and institutional inequities.

Countering a Colonizing Ideology

A fourth reason, less often used but no less important, to justify multicultural education is to counter a colonizing ideology. To understand this reason, you have to understand the process of colonization. Briefly, when one nation sought to colonize another, it often began by militarily dominating the people of that second nation. The primary goal of that domination was to exploit the natural resources of that nation, such as gold or oil, or the human resources of labor via the creation of slavery.

Usually this happened by a small group of powerful colonizers who inhabited a space among a very large group of people who were colonized. One way to solidify the domination and to make it easier for the powerful to maintain the colonization was to coerce the masses to accept domination and to believe that such domination was part of the natural order. Once the powerful dominated the minds of the masses, there was no need for a military presence. This colonization of the mind is arguably the worst aspect of the broader colonizing agenda.

The colonization of the mind happened in many ways but education was heavily implicated in this process. Schools began to teach the "glorious" history of the oppressor while simultaneously denigrating the history of the people of the nation. Holidays honored the heroes of the dominating class, their traditions became the new traditions of dominated, and the nation's story soon became one asserting that their domination was destiny.

Once again, anything from the colonized nation such as its heroes, its language, its traditions, and its resistance to colonization was made to appear backward, immoral, and worthless. Theories were developed and acted upon to explain the "deficiencies" of the colonized—lowered intelligence, dysfunctional families, destructive cultural values, useless languages, and on and on. These theories were employed to guide educational policies, were used to explain the colonized students' failures, and were taught within the walls of the school.

It is important to recognize that colonization happens not only from one nation to another, but that it can also happen within a nation. Such was the case in the United States where European Americans sought the colonization of those who first inhabited the lands of North America. All Indigenous peoples of the Americas, including Native Americans, Mexican-Americans, Hawaiians, and Alaskan Natives, have experienced this colonization within the United States. As with external colonization, colonization within the one's borders takes place in much the same way: the theft of natural and human resources, the development of an ideology to justify domination, and the dissemination of that ideology primarily via the education system.

While much of these explicit efforts to physically colonize are no longer evident today, the use of a Eurocentric curriculum (i.e., a Western European–focused curriculum) can still be described as an ongoing colonization of the mind. Importantly, often those who are teaching and those who are learning are not even aware that this curriculum is colonizing the mind.

The colonizing project continues on for people throughout their lives, since it is extended beyond school primarily by the media. It is difficult to work against this colonization, though an effort to describe and advance a *decolonizing* education is an important new contribution that can help advance multicultural education (as will be described later in this chapter).

Challenging Cultural Hegemony in Education

Another reason that teachers and scholars suggest we ought to pursue multicultural education is to counter cultural hegemony in education. Hegemony is when a powerful person, group, or nation exerts political, economic, cultural, or ideological control over another person, group, or nation, usually without the consent of the other(s). This power and control of one group over another rarely occurs via military force but rather through manufactured consent.[15]

Antonio Gramsci (1971) was the first to describe cultural hegemony. By this, Gramsci meant that in a society organized hierarchically by different social groups—by wealth or by other sociological characteristics such as race and ethnicity—the dominant group promotes policies and practices that seem as if they are neutral, logical, and natural. In addition, the values, beliefs, and behaviors of the dominating group or class of people come to be seen as normal, thus making all other ways of being deficient or deviant.

These norms, then, become so pervasive and systematized that oppressed peoples come to believe them as true as well. Upon closer inspection, these policies and practices benefit the dominant group and maintain its position of power and privilege. In this way, they are a form of racism operating within the structure of the society.

For Gramsci, education (more specifically civil society) and law (more specifically political society) are the primary means of state control.[16] Cultural hegemony is evident in education in many ways. Consider how often knowledge is understood to be neutral. As we described in Chapter 1, people create knowledge with all their biases, prejudices, political perspectives, and personal points of view that they have gained from their life experiences. Consider two books written about slavery and the Civil War: one by a historian from the South and one by a historian from the North. While both attempt to describe historical events objectively, one will leave out certain details the other would not. One would see an event and interpret it differently than the other.

As but another example of cultural hegemony in educational policy, consider the use of local property taxes to support local schools. On the face of it, this would seem logical, natural, and nondiscriminatory. However, the use of local property taxes privileges those in wealthy neighborhoods whose schools are heavily funded, as a result, in comparison to those in poor communities whose schools are significantly underfunded.

The result is stark differences in funding for schools in poor communities in comparison to more affluent communities. In *What Research Says about Unequal Funding for Schools in America*, Bruce Biddle and David Berliner (2003) point out that some of the wealthiest schools receive $16,000 per student while the poorest receive $4,000 per student. These funds impact everything from the quality of teachers who teach in these schools, to the quality of materials and resources available to them, to the quality of buildings where they work, as well as other aspects such as class size and support personnel.

Those who strive to dismantle inequities in their schools provide opportunities for students to question the way things have been, and continue to be, done in schools. For example, a teacher may encourage students to investigate a district's policy of testing students for English proficiency. Students could hone interviewing and researching skills, explore the history of educational testing, learn to interpret statistics and demographic information, and prepare a report or presentation for officials. These skills directly tie to several subjects.

Other important examples are taking place around the United States. For example, in some schools, students are learning the skills associated with ethnographic research as they focus on social problems in their own communities, in an effort to propose to policy makers solutions that will address these challenges.[17] In another instance, students are developing critical thinking habits associated with understanding public policy issues—such as immigration reform—and then leading community events where they share their understandings of these public policies with local community members.[18] While we will discuss these critical multicultural learning approaches more fully in Chapter 7, the important idea is that one goal of multicultural education is to help students realize that they can be actively engaged in addressing pressing social problems.[19]

Advocates believe that multicultural education can be used to challenge the cultural hegemony evident in schools and in the society. It can do so by first helping students to realize that the education curriculum is anything but neutral. It can also teach students to ask questions about the role of power and privilege when analyzing the roots of historical, political, cultural, or economic policies. That is, what multicultural advocates suggest to counter cultural hegemony is a distinctly political consciousness for both teachers and students. Such a critical consciousness leads to an empowering school culture.

Promoting Multicultural Education as a Human Right

The final justification for pursuing multicultural education is that it is a human right. Briefly, every student should have an opportunity to learn about himself/herself as an individual and as a member of various social groups. This would include students' group's history, their experiences with oppression or privilege, the contemporary issues facing their group, and the ways in which their group has combated oppression. It should include the many contributions that these groups have made to the nation. In effect, people should be able to see themselves in positive ways and members of their social group reflected in the schools where they learn.

A second reason why we assert multicultural education is a human right is its role in combating the scourge of prejudice and discrimination. As we are suggesting, addressing racism, classism, linguicism, etc.—cultural hegemony—is an important goal for multicultural educators. The devastating impact of racist, sexist, or homophobic comments can last a lifetime. Equally devastating can be denial of opportunities to learn, to earn and work, and to live in healthy ways that result from discriminatory behavior. We assert that every person has a right to live free from prejudice and discrimination. Multicultural education works toward that ideal.

A third reason why we see multicultural education as a human right is in its goal of helping students to learn about the lives and experiences of others. We often hear our students, when learning about the experiences of people different from themselves, exclaim that they "just didn't know." Learning about people different from oneself helps to understand them more fully, to appreciate who they are and what they bring to the spaces where they find themselves, and to value their cultural contributions to the nation and world.

The opportunity to hear and learn from multiple perspectives is a fourth reason why we see multicultural education as a human right. Just as people realize that it is always best to make decisions based on the widest variety of information available, so too should we provide students with the widest possible lens and knowledge to understand the social world around them. If teachers were only to tell the story of the victors, for example, students from that social group would have a distorted sense of their place in the world—as privileged, entitled, and superior to all others. Hearing multiple perspectives helps students learn about the complexity of life and provides a more complete, and thereby more accurate, picture of reality.

The final reason we advance for multicultural education as a human right is in its role to help students recognize their ability to influence the world. People are not only consumers of history. All people are participants and contributors of history. Students need to recognize that they can and must play an active role in pushing the nation to live up to its ideals enshrined in the nation's founding and living documents. A story of the United States is one of many people, working together, to make the most fundamental changes toward those democratic ideals. Young people have a right to help shape the future of this nation and to learn and experience the roles they can play to help this occur. As Amy Gutmann (1987) explains, "All citizens must be educated so as to have a chance to share in self-consciously shaping the structure of their society" (p. 46).

This critical awareness is closely linked to democratic practice and social justice.[20] However, multicultural education extends beyond preparing students for a participatory role in a democracy. As discussed in Chapter 1, creative democracy and multicultural democracy both demand recognition that diversity within democracy can move the nation as a whole toward a practical realization of democratic ideals. Instead of churning out like-minded individuals, many forms of multicultural education value diversity in both thought and action. Students who encounter such approaches to multicultural education develop supported opinions, respect the opinions and experiences of others, and strive to create opportunities for multiple perspectives to contribute to and flourish within society.

CURRENT CHALLENGES TO THE FIELD

As we consider the broader context that gives momentum to the field of multicultural education, we also recognize some powerful forces working against its promotion. Recall that multicultural education asserts that the broad purpose of education should be to prepare students for participation in a democracy. Thus any policies and practices need to be viewed and questioned with regard to that purpose. These include sorting, tracking, assimilating, and controlling nondominant group students. That is, multicultural education has critiqued past practices aimed at serving capitalist interests.

At the broadest level are public policies in the last couple of decades that have exalted capitalism and free-market reforms as the solution to all social challenges. Called neoliberalism, these policies seek to provide complete, unrestricted, and uncontrolled access of businesses to all facets of the society. Carole Edelsky (2006) described neoliberalism as "capitalism with the gloves off." The increasing influence of businesses in American public education has become evident in everything from television commercials in the classroom, to fast food and refreshments in the cafeteria, to for-profit schools themselves. For educators the irony is that these are the very same public policies—allowing businesses complete and unfettered control—that brought the U.S. economy to the brink of a world-wide recession.

Neoliberalist policies seek to challenge and change the emergence of the view of education from a social good in the public interest of an educated and engaged democratic population—one in which every person should be concerned about the education of every child given the implication for the overall health and vitality of the nation—to education as a private commodity to be bought and sold. Rather than thinking about education in the preparation of the next generation of this nation's participants, education has become a marketplace where individuals "buy" education that is fast, cheap, and easy. Education is increasingly seen as a commodity for individual consumption and job preparation for the global marketplace.

A related challenge to the multicultural education is the conservative opposition to multicultural education along with any other efforts to redress discrimination and pursue social justice. Some of the most evident ways in which this opposition has played out has been in court cases, most recently against efforts to promote student integration in Kentucky and Seattle, which have ruled against voluntary integration plans. But it is also evident in legislation to ban ethnic studies in Arizona and bilingual education in California, Arizona, and Massachusetts. It is evident in attacks on affirmative action. Collectively, these signal a shift toward pre-civil rights era policies and away from those policies that were put in place in the 1960s to 1980s to alleviate educational and social inequality.

A third challenge is the move toward standards and standardizing curriculum and instruction. While few would argue that schools ought not to have standards for themselves and their students, the question becomes who determines which standards should be adopted. The concern is that the standards adopted reflect a Eurocentric worldview. Anita Bohn and Christine Sleeter (2001) have argued that the standards movement has been a way to solidify that a Eurocentric curriculum dominates in schools and classrooms.

Connected with this movement is the standardization of curriculum and instruction. An increasing number of schools have gone to a scripted curriculum, which dictates what teachers should do and say. Teachers are then instructed that they need to be faithful to the curriculum, prohibiting any deviation that might be helpful for making more meaningful connections with learners. External consultants are employed or curriculum coaches are appointed to "help" these teachers to enact the curriculum but who often serve as curriculum police to assure teachers' faithfulness. Recognize that the restriction of choice (i.e., scripted curriculum) and surveillance of people (i.e., curriculum police) are two mechanisms of colonization.[21]

Some of the challenges to multicultural education are occurring within the field itself. Cameron McCarthy (1988), for example, has argued that from the beginning multicultural education was an attempt to appease nondominant culture communities who were agitated by the low academic performance of their youth. It never was, in his view, meant to substantially reform how schooling gets enacted for nondominant culture students.

It is also undermined by scholars who engage in multicultural education-oriented scholarship but whose analysis fails to address issues of power and privilege or whose recommendations for practice only address curriculum and instruction and not broader schoolwide reforms. It is undermined by teacher education training that often partitions multicultural education into a single course with no follow through in the rest of the teacher education program or related field-based experiences. It is undermined by teachers who refuse to acknowledge students' cultural identities in their approach to teaching.[22] It is undermined by teachers who believe that bringing multicultural education into the classroom is too political, so they rely on superficial diversity connections instead.

The most visible evidence of all these challenges, as they come together, can be found in the 2001 reauthorization of federal funding for public schools titled the *No Child Left Behind Act* (NCLB). The most challenging elements of this legislation, as described above, include the development of standards, the provision of restricted curriculum programs, and the use of standardized testing as the only valued way to measure student achievement. With respect to measuring achievement, the irony is that many educators had moved away from the sole use of standardized exams due to their biased nature. No significant changes had been made to alleviate this critique yet the use of standardized assessments as *the* way to measure academic achievement became the hallmark of this new legislation.

What the most recent legislation accomplished was to specify what could be learned, how it should be taught, and how it was to be assessed. For those schools that fail to meet these standards as taught and assessed, public funds can be used for tutoring assistance from for-profit companies. Continual failure can lead to the schools being closed and the opportunity for profit-oriented business organizations to re-establish new schools. To be sure, educators who advocate an education that is multicultural were not invited to this decision-making table.

Along with these are some other factors challenging multicultural education as well. These include a general willingness and resistance of teachers to change from the ways in which they were taught. It includes the lack of mentorship and professional development models that focus on how to help teachers foster an education that is multicultural. It includes the lack of significant numbers of teachers who can serve as role models for the ways in which multicultural education, in its most ideal form, can be implemented. Finally, there are some other factors within the field itself—unanswered questions, contested perspectives, and competing ideological orientations—that work against itself.

NEW DIRECTIONS IN MULTICULTURAL EDUCATION

Fortunately, there are some new forces that are helping to support the work of multicultural educators. At the broadest are global movements, evident more strongly outside of the United States, against neoliberalism. These can be seen in everything from mass protests against international trade organizations to local actions against those companies that allow child labor to be exploited in the production of their products. These new directions include local forums that address the exploitation of world capitalism as well as the writings of scholars who attempt to uncover the chameleon nature of neoliberalism.

It can also be seen in calls for a global education justice movement. Jennifer Chan-Tiberghien (2004) describes this movement as one that sees concrete connections between educational justice (such as literacy for all, educational assistance, access to education for girls) and sustainable development, women's rights, children's rights, and access to food and basic medicine. New directions include strengthening the links between critical, social justice-oriented schooling such as education for critical consciousness and social action. These new directions include cognitive justice such as valuing differing knowledges and ways of knowing. Finally it includes decolonizing methodologies such as approaches to the development of knowledge that values the perspectives and voices of those who have traditionally been unheard.

Some of these other positive forces, such as critical race theory and especially the renewed effort to bring multicultural education back to its critical pedagogical roots as will be discussed in later chapters.

For now, we wish to draw attention to the work around decolonizing education and around expanding educational standards focused on peace, justice, and environmental goals. Importantly, the origins for both arise from Indigenous communities and from the perspectives of Indigenous peoples. The two general perspectives differ in that decolonization works in direct opposition to current educational policies while the peace, justice, and environmental education standards movement seeks to reshape current policies.

Decolonization is an effort largely spurred by Maori scholars who wanted to push against the colonization that they experienced in Aotearoa/New Zealand. Briefly, there are two important steps associated with decolonization. The first is to recognize, critique, and then begin to delegitimize the superiority of the colonizing knowledge and ideologies that have been ingrained in both the individual and social psyche. The second, and perhaps the most important, is the recognition, restoration, and revitalization of the knowledges, cultural values, linguistic abilities, and historical events that sustained Indigenous peoples for hundreds of years prior to their colonization. Simultaneously, decolonization looks to that very community of indigenous peoples for guidance about modern-day adaptations in keeping with those cultural values.

A second important force in the field is a collection of educators who are advancing transformative standards that have a peace, social justice, and environmental sustainability focus to them. Their thinking and their proposals can be found in the book titled *Social Justice, Peace and Environmental Education.*[23] In essence, this group agrees that students, teachers, schools, and communities must have academic standards, but that these standards must be refocused away from basic skill, fact-recall, and job training motivations. For them, a more transformative set of standards would, "challenge the Standards movement and redirect the educational discourse away from exclusively academic accountability to a broader definition of accountability that embraces social justice, peace, and environmental justice" (p. 304).

Several groups, including Kauapa Maori and those Indigenous people who made up the Alaska Rural Systemic Initiative, have advanced standards that support their sovereignty, language, and culture so that their communities and the members who live there can thrive. These standards include principles for creating learning experiences through the local culture. In general these standards include educating young people to understand the full complexity of social injustices plaguing the globe. But they also call for helping young people learn the skills and develop the dispositions required to address these social and environmental challenges in ways that are creative and collaborative.

* * *

In sum, this is the broader context—global, national, and local—that multicultural education finds itself. It is the town, the village, the reservation, or the barrio in which the house of multicultural education is situated. Some of these influences work against multicultural education while some of the influences work to sustain it and help it to progress and renew.

For better and worse, like any community where we find ourselves, this is the landscape impacting multicultural education efforts. As important, we can and must play a role in helping to shape the context and places where we find ourselves. In essence, the vibrancy of the multicultural education house is connected to the broader community in which it finds itself.

NOTES

1. U.S. Department of Education, n.d.
2. National Center for Education Statistics, 2010a.
3. National Center for Education Statistics, 2010b.
4. See Gay, 2000, and Nieto & Bode, 2008 for more regarding multicultural education and the achievement gap.
5. U.S. Department of Education, n.d.
6. National Center for Education Statistics, 2010c.
7. Gewertz, 2010.
8. Bureau of Labor Statistics, 2010.
9. Valenzuela, 1999.
10. Spring, 2009.

11. See Gay, 2000 for more on incorporating multicultural education and multimodal instruction as a means to validate cultural identities.
12. See Nieto & Bode, 2008 and Sleeter & Grant, 2009 for more on enhancing cultural competence and inter-cultural communication.
13. See, for example, Hains, Lynch, & Winton, 2000.
14. Gay, 2000.
15. For a more detailed definition, see Gramsci, 1971.
16. See Brown, 2009 for a greater description of hegemony and educational law.
17. Duncan Andrade, 2008.
18. Cammarota & Romero, 2009.
19. See Banks & McGee Banks, Nieto & Bode, 2008 and Sleeter & Grant, 2009 for more on encouraging students to recognize and critique injustice.
20. See Nieto & Bode, 2008 and Sleeter & Grant, 2009 for more regarding the importance of multicultural education in the practice of democracy.
21. See MacGillivray, Ardell, Curwen, & Palma, 2004.
22. Milner, 2007.
23. Andrzejewski, Baltodano, & Symcox, 2009.

Chapter 3

The Streets and Paths

Principles of Multicultural Education

After developing an understanding of the broader layout of multicultural education, we can begin to explore the more specific streets and paths that provide frameworks for our own teaching and involvement in schools and communities. The focus of this chapter is to introduce those different paths that lead to an education that is multicultural.

Although the primary reasons to implement multicultural education (see Chapter 2) are often common across the various approaches, it is important to recognize the dynamic and complex nature of those approaches. As we emphasized in the Introduction to this book, there are many distinct paths that lead to an education that is multicultural. These paths or approaches may or may not intersect with others, they range in terms of ease of navigation, and they encounter unique obstacles.

In this chapter, we discuss several of the paths currently central to the field of multicultural education, including views outlined by Sonia Nieto and Patty Bode (2008), James Banks and Cherry McGee Banks (2010), Christine Sleeter and Carl Grant (2009), and Geneva Gay (2000). Despite their similarities, the paths demonstrate the complexity and choices educational stakeholders—those people who have indirect or direct interests in schools, including parents, teachers, administrators, and school board members—face as they set out down the road of multicultural education.

The last section of this chapter will describe a fork in that road. One branch supports the status quo of education and moves away from education that advances the values of democracy, while the other, a critical multicultural education pathway, promotes transformation and social change rooted in critical thinking and democratic principles.

SEVEN CHARACTERISTICS OF MULTICULTURAL EDUCATION

In their book, *Affirming Diversity: The Sociopolitical Context of Multicultural Education*, Sonia Nieto and Patty Bode (2008) define multicultural education as:

> A process of comprehensive school reform and basic education for all students. It challenges and rejects racism and other forms of discrimination in schools and society and accepts and affirms the pluralism (ethnic, racial, linguistic, religious, economic, and gender, among others) that students, their communities, and teachers reflect. Multicultural education permeates the schools' curriculum and instructional strategies, as well as the interactions among teachers, students, and families, and the very way that schools conceptualize the nature of teaching and learning. (p. 346)

Nieto and Bode expand on this definition arguing that multicultural education encompasses seven basic characteristics. First, it is *anti-racist*. Multicultural education attends to students' cultural backgrounds; responsive teachers and other stakeholders do not assume that all students are the same and that their experiences, based on their social identities, are unimportant.

Instead, multicultural education recognizes and addresses topics of racism and discrimination. The attempt is not to have other students feel guilty, which potentially stops a person from taking action; multicultural education is grounded in the hope and purpose for a biased-free society. For example, students might explore racial profiling for people from nondominant cultural groups, seeking the ways in which this profiling may be related to bias, and advancing recommendations for decreasing such profiling. Such work is grounded in hope and purpose.

A second characteristic of multicultural education, according to Nieto and Bode, is that such education is *basic education*, and therefore it should be considered as important as reading, writing, math, and technology education. Instead of focusing exclusively on a narrow body of knowledge, multicultural education values the dynamic and multi-dimensional knowledge systems of diverse peoples. For example, a school that recognizes the basic importance of multicultural education might engage faculty and staff in professional development that focuses on expanding all curricular areas to include multicultural content. As a result, students at this school would encounter more comprehensive and innovative perspectives than students attending a school utilizing more traditional approaches.

In addition to recognizing the basic, inherent value of multicultural education, Nieto and Bode argue that such basics are *important for all students*. Because multicultural education is more comprehensive than a monocultural education, it holds particular value as rigorous, meaningful learning. While such education is important in validating the cultural identities of non-dominant culture students, it is just as important for dominant culture students given the country's democratic foundations, the shifting demographics, and the need for educational innovation.

Schools that recognize this characteristic infuse their curriculum with multicultural content. For example, a school might require all students to complete advanced coursework focused on multiculturalism in order to graduate. Many colleges and universities have formally recognized the importance of diversity-focused coursework by requiring multicultural coursework for all students, regardless of major.

Since multicultural education is basic education and should be available to all students, Nieto and Bode also explain that it must be *pervasive*. Instead of isolated lessons, courses, or references, effective multicultural education extends across all subject areas and throughout the course of the entire school year. In addition to the academic influence, multicultural education must also permeate physical aspects of the school. As a result, multicultural education becomes a way of thinking—a philosophical perspective—as opposed to segregated or fragmented programs.

Along these lines, Nieto and Bode emphasize that responsive education is a *process*; it is dynamic, ongoing, and not something that can be checked off a list once a year. In order to recognize the philosophical and procedural orientation of multicultural education, teachers might partner with each other across grade levels and content areas to map and analyze multicultural content and the representation of diverse cultures throughout the school. Throughout the year (and subsequent years), team members might revisit the process, evaluate the results, and revise approaches and materials to reflect the dynamic nature of multiculturalism in the community and nation.

Nieto and Bode advocate for multicultural education that promotes *social justice* and *critical pedagogy*. In general, teachers who utilize responsive education must engage in self-reflection while also cultivating opportunities for students to develop social action skills. Such education does not accept the status quo, and it does not result simply in the transfer of low-level knowledge. Instead, responsive education pushes against injustice and engages students and communities to share various knowledge systems. For example, administrators might work with community leaders to identify injustices that exist within the current school system and to brainstorm ways to eliminate those injustices, and students might compile historical accounts based upon interviewing community members in order to challenge textbook depictions.

THE DIMENSIONS OF MULTICULTURAL EDUCATION

Nieto and Bode's definition is a helpful beginning for people thinking about multicultural education. James Banks and Cherry McGee Banks (2010) provide another perspective, another path, for those interested in fostering an education that is multicultural. For Banks and Banks, five dimensions further define schooling from a multicultural education perspective. The first is *content integration*. This implies that educational professionals infuse content and examples from various cultural groups throughout the entire school curriculum to support student learning. For example, a language arts teacher might assure that literature from many different social groups is part of the curriculum students encounter.

The second dimension outlined by Banks and McGee Banks is that of *knowledge construction*. This dimension focuses on guiding students through the analysis of their own thinking, and the thinking of others, in terms of cultural information. Such thinking requires learners to engage in the construction of knowledge in authentic and meaningful ways. In other words, students use processes used by real historians, scientists, etc. For example, a history teacher might encourage her students to critique their American history textbooks in terms of the portrayal of African Americans. Afterward, the teacher might share examples of primary documents related to the role of African Americans in the military during the Civil War and then ask students to rewrite a section of a chapter in the history book based upon those experiences.

Third, Banks and McGee Banks emphasize the role of *equity pedagogy*. Teachers who draw upon this dimension modify their instructional strategies and other pedagogical approaches to meet the needs and expectations of diverse students. For example, a teacher might utilize cooperative learning activities in order to better align with the traditional ways of sharing knowledge of students who are Native American.

The fourth dimension shared by Banks and McGee Banks focuses on *prejudice reduction*. Within this dimension, teachers facilitate learning that encourages students to confront their own inherent and learned biases. For example, a teacher might facilitate an exercise where students identify their understanding of their own cultures and share those understandings with other students. Then, the students might be asked to explore how people from their social group have been treated historically and contemporarily by the broader society.

The fifth and final dimension of multicultural education, as defined by Banks and McGee Banks, centers upon *empowering school culture*. In order to achieve this, schools, communities, and teachers must examine their practices to promote equity. For instance, a committee consisting of community members, teachers, students, and administrators might review course offerings to determine representation of diverse groups in curricular materials. The committee might also address the degree to which all students are provided meaningful opportunities to participate in all aspects of the school, from student council and extra-curricular activities to advanced, college-preparation courses.

In addition to offering these dimensions as a means to expand the definition of multicultural education, Banks and McGee Banks suggest that content integration, as described above, consists of four developmental levels when placed within the context of multicultural education. The *contributions approach* focuses on including cultural heroes, festivals, arts, and food within the traditional curriculum. These examples usually comprise a small, often stereotypical segment of the larger, mainstream curriculum. For example, students might learn about Black History Month by reading about George Washington Carver, Rosa Parks, and President Obama.

The second level of curriculum integration is the *additive* level, where a unit or content item is added to the mainstream curriculum without significantly altering the overall content. For example, as a part of a Coming of Age literature unit, a teacher might include a book about a young Native American boy's experiences growing up on a reservation.

Banks and McGee Banks describe the third level of curriculum integration as the *transformative* level. It is at this level that curriculum is altered to present multiple perspectives, which encourages students to critique knowledge traditionally included in textbooks and other content materials. Multicultural examples are integrated in comprehensive ways throughout the entire curriculum. For instance, students might study Westward Expansion by reading primary documents from migrants, missionaries, Native American leaders, newly freed slaves, and Chinese railroad laborers.

The fourth level of the model outlined by Banks and McGee Banks hinges upon *social action*. Students in this level engage in analyzing, critiquing, developing, and sharing curriculum. Multicultural examples are often at the center of learning at this level. For example, students might learn about immigration reform by interviewing migrant families, employers, and business owners in their community. They might then present a compilation of community members' stories to the state legislature in order to propose expanded bilingual education in their state.

Chapter 3

FIVE APPROACHES TO MULTICULTURAL EDUCATION

In their book *Making Choices for Multicultural Education: Five Approaches to Race, Class, and Gender*, Christine Sleeter and Carl Grant (2009) outline paths that support multicultural education to some extent, as well as a non-approach—the "business as usual" perspective. These approaches, like the curriculum integration levels outlined by Banks and McGee Banks, evolve in terms of comprehensiveness, respect for diversity, and cultivation of democratic values.

The first orientation Sleeter and Grant describe is the *business as usual* perspective. Within this view, teachers gravitate toward how and what they were taught as students, schools and states encourage standardization, and learning focuses on basic skills and facts. In general, educational maintenance becomes the focus of the learning, which is decontextualized from the community and cultural experiences of diverse students. Mainstream (White, middle class, Christian, heterosexual) values and experiences are central in such an approach.

Schools that utilize the *business as usual* approach may organize students into groups based upon cultural or linguistic background, gender, socioeconomic class, or ability level. Teachers who utilize this perspective may claim they do not see a students' cultural background and may believe they treat all students equally, even if they know students have unique experiences and needs. For example, nondominant culture students at a school adhering to the *business as usual* model might be underrepresented in advanced courses where engaging and rigorous content is paired with cutting-edge technology. Instead, the nondominant culture students might receive basic, drill and kill instruction in a substandard classroom.

Closely related to the *business as usual* perspective, Sleeter and Grant describe the approach that focuses on *teaching the exceptional and culturally different*. The goal of this model is to help diverse students assimilate into the mainstream society after providing short-term, intensive support services. Often, students receive such support through specialized courses and programs as a means to help them develop the "cultural capital"[1] necessary to succeed in the larger society. This cultural capital centers upon English fluency, math skills, written literacy, and understanding of Euro-American content (such as history, art, politics), so placement in remedial courses and special support programs often hinges upon test scores, English proficiency, and teacher referrals.

This model often assumes that diverse students are deficient and that in order to succeed they must assimilate into mainstream culture. For example, students who do not pass a test of English proficiency might be placed in an English as a Second Language (ESL) course for three semesters. In this course, they might learn basic English, and they also might learn about general American culture. The goal is not for the students to stay in the ESL program for their entire educational careers, it is not to develop in-depth understanding of English, and it is not to cultivate cultural identity or sustain first-language proficiency. Instead, the goal is to transition to a "regular" classroom within the shortest possible amount of time.

Sleeter and Grant suggest that the *human relations* approach begins to recognize and value the experiences of diverse students, as opposed to ignoring or segregating them. The goal of this model is to promote tolerance, effective communication, and the importance of acceptance both within the school and within the larger society. Many schools utilize this model to some degree, especially with increased attention given to cooperative learning, anti-bullying initiatives, and service education.

Teachers who use this approach may include isolated units or lessons that focus on the contributions of diverse peoples to the larger American society. While these lessons are potentially fragmented, there might be several, potentially complimentary or thematically intertwined initiatives focusing on a common message, such as managing conflict based on socioeconomic differences. As an illustration, students might participate in food drives in order to learn about people who are poor in the community.

Next, Sleeter and Grant describe an approach they term *single-group studies*. In general, this approach recognizes that education, historically, has not been neutral. The goal of this model is to recognize a specific cultural group and the common historical and cultural characteristics that define the group's identity. While such an approach focuses on one group at a time, the hope is that students will realize that other social groups have equally deep cultures.

Teachers who utilize this approach may teach entire courses or units devoted to the experiences of a specific cultural group, including the history of oppression, actions to oppose that oppression, contemporary issues facing the group, and contributions of the group to the broader society. While ideally such an approach would be available to all students, it is often seen within elective settings. For example, schools might offer coursework in Chicano art, African literature, or Indigenous government.

The next approach outlined by Sleeter and Grant, *multicultural education*, takes a more comprehensive stance. This approach focuses on diversity, cultural pluralism, and multiple perspectives, so teachers may address traditional academic concepts from several perspectives. In addition, community members may be involved in the development of curriculum, instruction, and assessment; task forces may work to assess equity in curricular, co-curricular, and extra-curricular contexts; stakeholders may strive to recruit and retain faculty and staff from nondominant cultural communities; and teachers may critique existing curricular materials for gender or cultural bias. To demonstrate this approach, students might compare the experiences of Jewish Europeans, Japanese Americans, Navajo code talkers, and Euro-American women using literature circles to study literature about World War II.

Sleeter and Grant describe a final approach, *multicultural social justice education*, which moves beyond recognizing and respecting difference to an active promotion of cultural pluralism, social change, and justice. Within this approach, teachers may focus instruction on justice-oriented topics (i.e. racism, disability studies, etc.) by drawing upon experiences from multiple perspectives. Community members and other educational stakeholders may be extensively involved throughout the planning and evaluation phases.

In general, schools and classrooms that support *multicultural social justice education* function as democratic entities, where students and communities advance change. For example, students might work in teams to identify, document, and respond to a community challenge. Throughout their in-depth coursework, they might learn to apply skills from a variety of academic disciplines as they prepare their solution-oriented presentations for community organizations. As a result of the project, students might demonstrate application of research, interviewing, mathematical, technological, and writing skills through the gathering, interpretation, and representation of data.

CULTURALLY RESPONSIVE PEDAGOGY

A final multicultural education path, outlined by Geneva Gay (2000), describes "culturally responsive pedagogy" for educators and education professionals. Gay argues that responsive pedagogy consists of four aspects: caring, communication, curriculum, and instruction.

The first aspect, *caring*, centers upon action. Teachers and other stakeholders must go beyond saying they care about students—they must *show* that they care for students by validating cultural ways of knowing. In addition, *caring* includes setting high expectations for learning. Such rigor must be multidimensional, so responsive, caring teaching should infiltrate all aspects of education. Finally, responsive educators and educational stakeholders demonstrate their ability to care by actively learning from their students and communities and by engaging in ongoing dialogue and reflection. For example, caring teachers might attend extracurricular and community events, dialogue with students about interests, and incorporate those interests into learning opportunities.

Gay also emphasizes the importance of effective *communication* as a component of culturally responsive education. Responsive educators and other stakeholders recognize that there are multiple ways of knowing and of sharing one's knowledge; they also realize that communication about knowledge is shaped by culture, experience, and identity. Such teachers create a space for students to utilize culturally responsive approaches to task completion, problem solving, taking positions, and experimenting. As a result, students are not forced to choose between academic success and cultural values. For example, a teacher might incorporate many forms of literacy into his/her teaching, including visual, kinesthetic, and digital forms. He/She might emphasize that there are many ways to share information and stories, and that those different ways should meet the needs of the sharer and the audience.

Gay also emphasizes the importance of responsive *curriculum*, given its role in advancing academic achievement for all students—especially nondominant culture students. Textbooks and other curriculum materials must be selected carefully with the help of community and cultural leaders, students, and parents. It is also important to note that responsive curriculum extends beyond sharing a few contributions of diverse groups; it focuses upon the histories, experiences, perspectives, and issues relevant to the group. Curricular resources come from a variety of sources, including community-based sources. Most importantly, students engage in the critical examination of curriculum. For example, students might engage in community-based learning and curricular critiques that result in presentations to textbook publishers, stakeholders, and educators from around the country.

In addition, Gay focuses on the importance of responsive *instruction*. Responsive educators and other stakeholders recognize and value a variety of learning modalities, so they work to integrate culture and language into instruction in comprehensive ways. As a result, such schools utilize active, cooperative learning, alternative literacies, technology, and a variety of instructional approaches. For example, instead of standing over students while lecturing from the front of the classroom, a responsive teacher might move around the classroom as students work in teams to solve problems and create projects.

We provide a general overview of how these different conceptions of multicultural education overlap and support each other in Table 3.1. Identifying the ways in which these different theories support common concepts makes it clearer what scholars in the field find as most essential to understanding multicultural education.

Table 3.1   Concepts and Approaches to Multicultural Education

Concepts	Nieto & Bode (2008)	Sleeter & Grant (2009)	Gay (2000)	Banks & McGee Banks (2010)
Cross-Cultural Responsiveness	• Anti-Racist • A Process	• Human Relations	• Caring Relations • Communications	• Prejudice Reduction
Equity Pedagogy (Instruction)		• Teaching the Culturally Different	• Culturally Responsive Instruction	• Equity Pedagogy
Responsive Curriculum	• Basic Education		• Responsive Curriculum	• Content Integration
Critical Consciousness	• Critical Pedagogy	• Group Studies		• Knowledge Construction
Empowering School Culture	• Pervasive • For All	• Multicultural Education		• Empowering School Culture
Democratic, Social Justice Education	• Social Justice	• Multicultural Social Justice Education		

CRITICAL MULTICULTURAL EDUCATION

Although countless paths lead toward multicultural, democratic education to some extent, there is extensive variation in the level of application and transformation that results from walking the different paths. To be sure, some educators are just beginning and are taking their initial steps toward an education that is multicultural. It is helpful, however, to see where more rigorous, critical approaches can lead educators. Still, it can be overwhelming to make practical sense of even the most popular definitions and models. In general, most multicultural education theorists explain that there are five general types of education in terms of multiculturalism, each type progressively more democratic and transformative than the previous level:

• Education that ignores multiculturalism altogether;
• Education that views multiculturalism as an obstacle to success in mainstream society;
• Education that values multiculturalism in terms of contributions to the mainstream society;

- Education that comprehensively recognizes and values multiculturalism; and,
- Education that encourages students to engage in promoting multiculturalism and democratic values.

It is important to recognize that most efforts to expand multicultural education continue to fall short of the more transformative, comprehensive, and meaningful approaches. Often, teachers and schools who strive to expand multicultural education, especially initially, end up utilizing superficial techniques. They add a Latina/o literature unit, they create a school-wide Native American History Day, or they ask students to come to school with a food item traditional to their cultural background. While all of these examples, if done authentically and respectfully—in ways that do not reinforce stereotypes—may be better than not engaging in multicultural education at all, they are often short-lived, fragmented, and decontextualized.[2] Genuine multicultural education must extend across subjects, days, and courses. It must also go beyond what teachers teach to include *how* they teach and *why* they teach.

It is this *why* of teaching that sets critical multicultural education apart from other forms of multicultural education. For teachers, students, and other stakeholders, critical multicultural education provides a way to engage in democratic practice, investigate meaningful topics, and strive to advance change in real schools and communities.

Stephen May and Christine Sleeter (2010) note that multicultural education has faced many setbacks in recent years. Despite decades of advocacy for multicultural education, teachers continue to view their "minoritized" students as deficient (p. 3). The authors argue that these setbacks result from a lack of serious and systematic attention to *critical* multicultural education. In other words, the authors explain that too often educators and policy makers apply multicultural education in superficial ways that send a clear message to both nondominant culture and mainstream students: We adults do not really believe in the importance of multicultural education.

May and Sleeter also emphasize a disconnect between theory and practice, citing a lack of specific examples for educators and other stakeholders. However, the authors also caution the tendency of teachers and administrators to seek quick fixes to educational challenges. In terms of critical multicultural education, this tendency may itself encourage a superficial application.

For example, teachers working on a Native American reservation may latch onto methods suggested for Native children generally, instead of looking to the specific community for guidance. As a result, they ignore the variations between and within specific tribal communities, and they restrict their own ability to learn. In critical multicultural education, these aspects cannot be ignored. Instead of a trivialized effort to implement multicultural education, May and Sleeter emphasize the importance of teacher self-reflection, dialogue with community members and students, and acceptance of multicultural education as a dynamic process in which students *and* teachers must continuously evolve as learners.

How might this look in practice? One way to consider the theoretical principles that contribute to critical multicultural education is to view the ideas within the context of content areas. In general, critical multicultural education should:

- Include various forms of literacy,
- Engage students in social or political action,
- Acknowledge the role of discomfort in transformative learning,
- Recognize multiple ways of knowing, and,
- Connect to cultural expertise.

For example, within the context of language arts instruction, critical multicultural education *emphasizes various forms of literacy*. Teachers, then, might encourage students to explore spoken word poetry and hip-hop lyrics as a means to expand understanding of literacy development, as opposed to focusing exclusively on written texts or works created by Euro-American writers.

Another characteristic of critical multicultural education is that it should *engage students in social and/or political action*. Within the context of math, for example, students might analyze data from Hurricane Katrina and consider the implications for different ways of sharing data with the public. As a result of such a project, future media coverage of similar events, even on a local level, might lead to improved response efforts.

To advance critical multicultural education, it is important to *recognize the role of discomfort in transformative learning*. For mainstream learners, this means that responsive teachers may encourage participant discomfort on some level. For example, within the field of social studies, students might engage in open-ended, ongoing small group discussions about privilege as associated with gender, race, religion, class, etc. Such conversations may generate initial feelings of guilt or anger, but through continued examination, they can lead to high-level analysis of complex concepts.

Since critical multicultural education *recognizes and values multiple ways of knowing*, it is important that students engage in the exploration of various knowledge systems when learning about the world, history, and themselves. Within the study of scientific disciplines, for example, students might encounter oral histories about the use of native medicinal plants by Indigenous peoples as they explore biological diversity in their community.

Drawing upon the cultural expertise of students and community members is another essential attribute of critical multicultural education. Community members might participate as co-teachers in the classroom. Within the arts, students might utilize digital storytelling, theater, or film to document community issues and perceptions in order to share interpretations with authentic audiences.

Throughout this chapter, we provided real examples to help make the theory approachable for the various stakeholders in the field. However, it is important to realize that these are simply examples—there are countless ways to implement critical multicultural education in your own communities. It is also important to note that given the dynamic nature of multicultural education, there is no end to the journey. The path continues, and stakeholders should avoid walking it simply to reach a destination.

* * *

We can choose to walk countless paths when it comes to multicultural education. Despite this, educational decision makers face two main roads at the onset of their journey to educate students. In the end, we must look beyond basic but often superficial approaches to multicultural education in order to advance learning for today's diverse students.

One road leads away from cultural responsiveness, diversity, and equity. That road follows the same route outlined by decades of educational policy and ignores the importance of truly valuing and advancing diversity in and beyond schools. It is a well-traveled road, and one that is popular and easily followed. Despite its popularity, it is a road of privilege, and it does not support the journeys of all students. If we choose that road, we close access gates for many of our students.

The other road, a less traveled and less familiar one, leads toward responsive, critical education and opportunity for all students. This road winds through uncharted lands and into the heart of the communities—both established and emergent—that surround our schools. Although it is rougher going, this critical multicultural education road is open to all travelers. It is a road of transformation and justice.

NOTES

1. See Bourdieu & Passeron, 1977. Also, see Banks, & McGee Banks, 2010 and Nieto & Bode, 2008.
2. Gorski, 2008b and Tellez, 2002 argue that these token efforts can never be done effectively.

Chapter 4

The Walls

Multicultural Education to Combat Oppression and Resistance

The 2008 U.S. presidential election of Barack Obama was historic on many counts. It was an election that was built on grassroots organizing, especially by young people, which used new technologies to get the message out about his campaign platform. It was an election that brought the most diverse groups of people together—Blacks and Whites, young and old, urban and suburban—to vote for Obama. And it was historic for this nation to elect its first biracial (African American and White) person to the nation's highest political office.

The election of President Obama led to a national dialogue about race relations in the United States. For some, this election heralded the end of racism as a defining feature of American society. After all, a majority of voters had elected a biracial president. Some even suggested that the United States, with this election, had moved to a "post-racial" era. To be sure, this was an important victory and a significant symbol that the United States had advanced in terms of inter-racial relations.

However, the idea of a post-racist society in the United States has not been universally agreed upon. In fact, many argue that racial tensions have grown even more troubling in recent years. This is true for both explicit forms of racism as well for those less obvious forms of racism. In fact, Jesse Washington (2008) of the Associated Press noted a particularly high spike in racially motivated attacks—from calls to assassinate Obama, to crosses being burned on the lawns of Obama supporters, to the physical attack by White youths shouting Obama while beating an African American youth—as a result of Obama's election to the presidency. In 2008, the Southern Poverty Law Center noted an increase in the number of hate groups within the United States to an all time high of 926 (up from 888 a year earlier).[1]

Beyond these obvious forms of racism are the various ways in which racism has become less obvious but as troubling just the same. Edward Bonilla-Silva (2003) calls this "racism lite" or "racism with a smile." Scholars describe these as micro-aggressions. Such examples include all the subtle and sometimes even unconscious ways in which racism rears its ugly head. It could be a slight on a person's qualifications such as "She's really smart for being a woman." It could be playing out a stereotype that a person grew up believing such as, soon after meeting a Latina/o person, mentioning that Mexican food is one's favorite. Or, it could be simply deciding to sit next to a group of White students but away from an African American group of students. As suggested, these less obvious—or implicit—forms of racism are often more revealing of race relations than the more explicit forms in terms of recognizing racism in the United States.

While demographic changes, academic performance challenges, and cultural competency development continue to be important reasons why multicultural education might be enacted, so too is the need to combat colonization and hegemony (as discussed in Chapter 2). Rooted in both of these are the ideological underpinnings, including racism, that serve these interests.

THE WALLS OF THE HOUSE OF MULTICULTURAL EDUCATION

The first things that people notice as they come upon a house are the walls. On walls, both negative and positive things are written: racist or sexist graffiti or, like the murals in some nondominant cultural communities, positive, bold images that tell the community's story from its point of view. On the walls of multicultural education are written those forms of oppression and the resistance to that oppression that serve as the impetus for multicultural education.

This chapter will advance the multicultural education ideal of pursuing harmony and promoting unity while combating prejudice and discrimination. To get at oppression in the forms of most interest to multicultural education, the chapter will describe four levels of racism: personal, institutional, societal, and epistemological. White privilege, as a manifestation of racism, will be described.

We then move to describing dysconscious racism, which is the acceptance of both racism and White privilege, followed by a more concrete description of the various forms that racism takes. Finally, since oppression does not remain uncontested, we will turn attention toward the various ways in which people resist oppression in school contexts. This includes everything from overt resistance, such as "willful not learning,"[2] to protest such as in the student walkouts of the 1970s, to resilience and perseverance in the face of such oppression.

OPPRESSION IN ITS VARYING FORMS

As we have noted in Chapter 1, the beginning foundations of multicultural education—ethnic studies—were directed at identifying and naming oppression in all its forms. That is, from the very beginning, multicultural education was rooted in understanding oppression. This was especially notable during the Intergroup Relations Movement of the late 1950s. It was during this time that the causes and consequences of stereotyping, prejudice, and discrimination served as a focal point. Since that time, attention to racism, sexism, classism, homophobia, and ableism has been a consistent and persistent thread throughout multicultural education.

One important change, however, since the Intergroup Relations Movement of the 1950s was the change from thinking about racism as an individual-to-individual action to thinking about its more structural and philosophical forms. This is called institutional racism.

Four Levels of Racism

Jim Scheurich and Michelle Young, in 1997, provided one of the clearest explanations of the various levels in which racism occurs. At the first level, the *personal* level, the focus is on the individual actions against another individual or group of individuals. This is the level most people consider when they think of bias and discrimination. This is due partly to the fact that an individualist orientation is a dominant worldview orientation for dominant culture people in the United States. It is also partly due to the fact that these forms of bias and discrimination are the most obvious: hearing a person make a homophobic remark, watching a co-worker rudely wait on a customer because of the color of his skin, or recommending only male students for a gifted and talented program even though the class consists of more female students. Given this individualist orientation, racism is understood as perpetrated by one biased individual and these individual actions are isolated.

We wish to be clear that our intent here is not to minimize the power of these individual forms of racism. In fact, we are interested in not only these actions in their most explicit forms but also as micro-aggressions as described earlier. However, in suggesting other levels to consider when attempting to understand and push against these forms of prejudice and discrimination, we argue that an individual's behavior is made possible by other levels at which prejudice and discrimination are operating.

A second level of prejudice and discrimination is that which plays out at the *institutional* level. Recall that colonization requires that the colonizers seize the mechanisms of the state and then shape them in ways that maintain the colonization. Thus this level of discrimination and prejudice is focused on the ways institutions—electoral systems, businesses, and schools—are structured and enact policies and practices that serve the interests of the dominant social group.

The decision, for example, to make English the language of instruction in New Mexico, shortly after the end of the Mexican-American War, and despite the fact that a supermajority of school-aged children spoke only Spanish, was one way to ensure that the members of the English-speaking dominating class would maintain their domination. This decision assured that their children would be most successful while those for whom English would be a new language were disadvantaged from the outset.

In schools, multicultural educators are concerned about a variety of institutional structures, policies, and practices that maintain educational inequality.[3] These include tracking, a Eurocentric curriculum, standardized exams (which have yet to prove they are either culture-free or culture-fair), retention in grades, disciplinary policies, school climate, and even the physical structure of school. But it also includes the ways students are disempowered in schools as well as including the ways caregivers and community members are distanced from meaningful connections with schools. Finally, given the current wave of mandated reforms from the state, it includes the ways even teachers are constrained to meet the needs of their students.

A third level of analysis is *societal*. This is the level at which groups within any nation vie and compete for the nation's ethos. Ethe (plural of ethos) are concerned with the characters, periods of time, and social contexts that influence the attitude and actions of the nation. Different social identity groups experience the nation's current ethos differently. The group in power then sets the agenda for the nation and fosters a particular national narrative or story about what it means to be American or what justice ought to mean, what equality entails, or what constitutes success.

Consider how bilingual education is perceived differently by most Euro-Americans in contrast to those views held by most Indigenous Americans, Latina/os, and Asian Americans. For example, while Whites voted to abolish bilingual education by 2 to 1 margin in California in 1998, nondominant culture voters voted to retain bilingual education by the same margin.[4]

The final level of analysis is the *philosophical* level. Of interest at this level are questions of epistemology. Epistemology refers to the exploration of theories of the nature of knowledge such as what counts as knowledge, whose knowledge is valued and worth knowing, how knowledge is shared and acquired, how people come to know, and how knowledge is assessed. All persons interested in education are profoundly impacted by questions of epistemology.

Epistemologies are racial and gendered. While there is a dominant racial and gendered epistemological orientation, there are other epistemologies that stand in contrast to this dominant orientation. Prejudice and discrimination are in place when the dominant group determines that its knowledge is more important than that of other groups, that some ways of coming to know (that is, learning) consistent with its value orientation are better than others, and that there is only one way of demonstrating what one knows consistent with the group's assessment preferences.

The privileging of knowledge, approaches to learning, and types of assessment leads to epistemological injustice, and such understanding led Scheurich and Young (1997) to raise questions, asked previously by nondominant culture members, about epistemological racism.

While the epistemological level is the most abstract, it is the most powerful since it sets the stage for what happens at the other three levels. That is, epistemological orientations are the foundation for the national narrative and societal ethos. These, in turn, are used to justify and explain institutional polices and practices so that they appear natural, normal, neutral, fair, and logical when in fact they exemplify institutional racism. Collectively, then, the ideologies, dominant national narrative, institutional policies, and practices set the stage for individual-to-individual prejudice and discrimination.

An Example

Consider this extended example. In 2008, the Superintendent of Public Instruction of the state of Arizona sought to ban the teaching of Mexican-American studies in the largely Latina/o schools of Tucson, Arizona. At the *individual level*, you could explain this as evidence of an overzealous, perhaps even racist, school administrator acting out his prejudices.

At the *institutional level* are policies and practices that give more weight to some content (math and literacy) than others (such as ethnic studies content), given what is assessed on the state wide academic achievement exam. It followed up on policies enacted earlier to abolish bilingual education and to ban teachers who spoke English with an accent. At the same time, there were other public policies being enacted that would allow police to question people about their immigration status and, when failing to produce proof of citizenship, this questioning could lead to arrest and immediate deportation.

At the *societal level*, the dominant narrative in the state at the time was one that included the belief that immigrants were overrunning the schools and state. Claims were being made that this ethnic studies curriculum was making students resentful as they learned about their history of oppression and forms of resistance used in the past.

At the *epistemological level*, a variety of beliefs serve as the foundation for these actions: nondominant group students need not to learn about the history and contemporary challenges of their social group; learning about one's social group has no academic value; learning about one's social group will result in disunity in the nation as students become resentful; a Eurocentric curriculum is the most essential knowledge base students can be taught; and, student critical thinking and engagement in social change is anathema to being a good person in Arizona.

The important point is that what occurred at the individual level was made *probable* by those things that occurred at the institutional, societal, and epistemological levels. That is, the institutional, societal, and epistemological levels shape, but do not determine, what happens at the individual level. For multicultural educators, then, the most important levels of analysis and the most important efforts directed at change need to occur at the institutional, societal, and epistemological levels.

White Privilege

Early in the 1900s, W. E. B. Du Bois (1935/1995) noted that not only were Blacks discriminated against, but also that Whites stood to gain simply because of the color of their skin even when these Whites were poor and working in low-wage conditions. That is, while he understood that Blacks were experiencing discrimination, he simultaneously recognized that Whites were privileged by this discrimination. He said:

> It must be remembered that the white group of laborers, while they received a low wage, were compensated in part by a sort of public and psychological wage. They were given public deference and titles of courtesy because they were white. They were admitted freely with all classes of white people to public functions, public parks, and the best schools. The police were drawn from their ranks, and the courts, dependent on their votes, treated them with such leniency as to encourage lawlessness. Their vote selected public officials, and while this had small effect upon the economic situation, it had great effect upon their personal treatment and the deference shown them. White schoolhouses were the best in the community, and conspicuously placed, and they cost anywhere from twice to ten times as much per capita as the colored schools. The newspapers specialized on news that flattered the poor whites and almost utterly ignored the Negro except in crime and ridicule. (pp. 700–701)

More contemporarily, others have taken the notion of the "public and psychological wage" paid to those who are White, seeking to question Whiteness and to uncover White privilege. While some could argue that this deflects attention away from racism and sexism, others see it as essential: There is a need to see it as the other side of the racism coin.

Paula Rothenberg's (2008) edited book *White Privilege*, for example, seeks to accomplish several goals. The first objective is to make Whiteness visible. This is because Whiteness is a kind of unspoken, unconscious, and tacit form of understanding social relations. For example, when White students are asked to describe their identity, they often will say they are "just American." They have come to equate their race with the identity of the nation. They have not learned the ways Whiteness has become a form of ethnocentrism—the measure by which all other things are determined.

Whites, in the main, are never confronted about being White and so they unconsciously assume their Whiteness is normal and natural. Race, then, is what other people have. When the White person is successful, he/she rarely will even consider that his/her Whiteness played a role in that success; thus it must be effort, motivation, talent, and skill that best explain the success.

Second, given the invisible power of Whiteness, and given that race is a social construct (that is, the society gives meaning to what it means to be a member of a particular social group based on certain physical traits such as color of skin), it should be no surprise that what it means to be White has changed over time. Equally interesting are questions about which groups count as White and how has certain groups sought to be classified as White when originally the society did not classify them as such. Jews, Greeks, Italians, and the Irish were such examples, excluded at first from being considered White and later included.

Third, discussions of Whiteness include detailing the ways in which Whiteness includes certain privileges. These are part of what Peggy McIntosh (2004) calls the "Invisible Knapsack" of unearned privileges she gains as a result of being White. These include things like never having to speak for your race, not being followed in grocery store by the in-store security officer, never having to wonder if someone moved out of the neighborhood because you moved in, being sure that when you ask to see the person in charge, you're likely to see someone who shares your same skin color, among many other examples of the nature of White privilege.

Last are discussions of using Whiteness to resist oppression of other groups and to develop alliances across racial lines. This comes about by those Whites who realize that they have gained much based on an unfair advantage and that these gains are unsatisfactory as a result. They are motivated, then, by fairness and justice.

As a result, these White allies use all they have to combat racism and to disrupt the privileges given out on the basis of race. This includes taking a strong anti-racist stance when evidence of discrimination is made visible. It includes using their Whiteness to question policies and practices that give unfair disadvantage to some groups and advantage to others. It means seeking out alternative social narratives, especially as told by nondominant culture people. Finally, it means seeking to broaden the epistemological beliefs underlying the ways in which we think about teaching, learning, knowing, and assessment.

Dysconscious and Passive Racism

One of the additional ideas that can be gleaned from this work by Rothenberg (2008) is the idea that people are often unaware of their own privileges, but they are also often unaware of the racism around them. Joyce King (1991) described this as dysconscious racism. For her, dysconscious racism is "an uncritical habit of mind . . . that justifies inequality and exploitation by accepting the existing order of things as given." It is different from those anti-racist individuals who are constantly questioning their own beliefs and actions while simultaneously working to oppose the marginalization of others. An important idea about this dysconsciousness is that nondominant culture people can also adopt it. That is, they can internalize racism.

Another key idea that emerges that we want to make explicit is that people can engage in the very difficult work of not being racist personally but still engage in passive racism. As defined, passive racism is evident when a person allows, either consciously or unconsciously, racist policies and practices to remain, or they fail to question the dominant narrative or the prevailing ideologies underlying it. Passive racism occurs when an individual does not engage in racist or sexist or homophobic behavior but remains silent in the face of those behaviors as exhibited by others. In essence, the claim is made that unless you are actively pushing against racism in all facets of living, you may be engaging in passive racism.

Valarie Ooka Pang (2005) provides but one other example of passive racism in her book *Multicultural Education: A Caring-Centered, Reflective Approach.* She states the following:

> Teachers avoid discussing incidents in which children call each other names that refer to race, class, gender physical differences, and religion. Teachers may not know how to talk about these incidents, but avoiding open discussion when children know the teacher heard the name-calling suggests that the

teacher does not object to the use of those terms. It is a passive acceptance of discrimination. (p. 182).

A Typology of Racism

Another way to consider and think about race and racism is to view it in its many forms. While several scholars have proposed such typologies,[5] a study done at one of our universities provided us with a glimpse at many of the ways in which racism plays itself out in the everyday lives of college students.[6] The study identified four main ways in which racism plays out and several specific formats within each. These four approaches fall within traditional forms of racism or within more modern (liberalism) approaches to racism.

The first traditional form of racism was titled *no doubt* racism. It is those actions that can be termed active racism. In these cases, individuals made prejudicial statements or stereotypical comments about people different from themselves. In addition, *no doubt* racism also included statements or actions that served to "Other" individuals—to make them appear foreign, not normal, and marginal.

A second form of traditional racism evident in this study was *segregation*. It included all the ways in which people segregate themselves from those individuals who are different. Sometimes this segregation is physical, as in who sits with whom in the school cafeteria. Of note is evidence that while White students will ask why nondominant culture students will sit together, the fact is that White students are more actively choosing to sit with other White students than are nondominant culture students choosing to sit with other students from nondominant cultural groups.[7] In essence, nondominant culture students make a more active effort to integrate; it is White students' behavior that best explains segregated seating arrangements.

This form of segregation included the ways students chose to stay away from the ideas and experiences of people from nondominant cultures, such as refusing to read books or hear about their experiences via college coursework. One final way this segregation plays itself out is in the discomfort these students feel when they are in the presence of any significant number of nondominant culture students.

The third and fourth cluster, termed *liberalism racism*, is rooted in the idea of Enlightened liberalism. It comes from the prevailing idea that the focus of attention should be on individual rights, on equality (treating everyone alike), and on meritocracy—the idea that an individual rises or falls on his/her own merit, ambition, motivation, skills, and talents. The converse is also true: if an individual fails, it is a result of lack of ambition, skill, and talent.

Liberalism refuses to look at institutional, societal, and ideological forces that might explain why two individuals—one White and one a nondominant culture person—who have the same motivation, skill, and talent might not succeed equally. One other element of racist liberalism is the claim of "colorblindness"[8]—that one does not see color. Besides being a psychological impossibility, individuals who assert that they do not see a person's color fail to acknowledge an important element of the identity of nondominant culture people—who they are racially, culturally, and ethnically.

Cluster three, then, of liberalism racism was titled revisionist racist narratives. In these university students' experiences, these were attempts to explain racist statements or actions as not racist at all. It also included attempts to justify why someone would make such statements but then state she/he did "not really mean anything negative" by them. A third manner in which this played out is evident in tokenism—claiming that a one is not racist since "one my best friends is" a person from a nondominant culture.

Cluster four is called equal opportunity racism. This was evident when individuals claimed that Whites, despite all the privileges and advantages they have as a product of being White, are the new victims of efforts at racial equity. Recall that equality (treating all individuals the same) is a hallmark of racist liberalism; hence any programs to provide uplift for nondominant culture people results in reverse racism. Given this new victimology, then, White students feel justified in being angry with people from nondominant cultures; for White students, it solidifies their prejudices and explains their discriminatory behaviors. At minimum, it fails to acknowledge the long history of racism in this country.

RESISTING RACISM AND OPPRESSION

We now turn attention to the ways in which individuals and different groups have opposed racism. Just as individuals are socialized into developing attitudes and behaviors that maintain current social inequality (at best) or promote that inequality via outright oppression (at worst), so too can they be socialized toward promoting liberation. It is interesting to note that rarely is resistance and liberation a part of the national discourse. Consider how often stories are left untold of those who worked actively to oppose their oppression and the allies who worked alongside them in these efforts.

Bobbie Harro (2000) has developed a model, called the "Cycle of Liberation," to demonstrate how you can move toward more libratory practices via confronting oppressive action. Briefly, it requires that you have a strong sense of self and a strong support base from which to operate. First, you begin by engaging in activities that serve as initial preparation such as taking courses related to racism, developing analytical skills, and/or integrating interpersonal skills related to cultural responsiveness as well as the skills to disrupt oppression. Most often, some critical incident occurs that then spurs you to want to take broader action.

Second, you reach out to others to understand their experiences and to begin to use the skills that you have developed. This phase includes building community via working with others who are both similar and different from you. It might include everything from engaging in fund raising activities, to political lobbying, to becoming an ally or refusing to take privilege.

Third, you and your allies begin to take action to change policies and practices that maintain social inequalities. This might include challenging assumptions, taking a leadership role, supporting others in their leadership work, and sharing power. This phase ends with working to maintain the gains made and inspiring hope and care for others.

Historically, many efforts were made, mostly by nondominant culture people, to oppose the oppression of the social groups to which they belonged. Consider how the work of intellectuals such as W. E. B. Du Bois actively sought to counter the prevailing negative discourse regarding African Americans at the turn of the century. Of course, during the Civil Rights period, there was active engagement against legal segregation as it played out in almost all facets of life in the United States.

While there were important leaders of this movement (Martin Luther King, Jr. and Rosa Parks, to name just two), the effort was mostly successful due to the heroic efforts of countless numbers of ordinary women, men, and children who actively opposed segregation as it occurred in everyday activity. They resisted via teach-ins, political rallies and marches, sit-ins, or outright refusal to accept living and learning in a segregated society. Recall that these women, men, and children were often met with the full force of the law: They were beaten with club sticks, dispersed by water hoses, or arrested and sent to jail. These were the real leaders of the Civil Rights Movement.

In addition, there have been important efforts on behalf of White anti-racist activists. Consider the role of the Highlander School in Tennessee, founded by Myles Horton and Don West. Originally founded as a center focused on workers' rights in the 1930s, the Highlander School turned its attention to issues of civil rights in the 1950s and 60s. It began a citizenship education program that sought to prepare African Americans to pass literacy exams required at the time to be able to vote. It included leadership training and hosted as its participants Martin Luther King, Jr., Rosa Parks, Septima Clark, and Ralph Abernathy. Contemporarily, there are organizations such as the Southern Poverty Law Center, Teaching Tolerance, and Race Traitors.

Students, historically and contemporarily, also have played an active role in resisting their oppression. As mentioned before, they were important actors during the Civil Rights Movement. That movement included school walkouts, called *blowouts* in the Latina/o community, which were used to call attention to inequality in schooling experience. These students protested the low representation of teachers from nondominant cultures, lack of opportunities to learn about themselves via ethnic studies courses, and the absence of bilingual education programs within the school walls. As important, today's students have walked out of schools, attended teach-in workshops, and marched on city streets in support of immigrant rights or to oppose bans on ethnic studies.

On a more personal level, when students are confronted with racial barriers in education, they resist that oppression in a variety of ways. One such way is called "willful not learning." Herbert Kohl (1994) identifies how students can just shut down, choosing not to learn things that violate their integrity and identity. Note that all people engage in some form of "willful not learning": Most people choose not to learn to sell drugs, choose not to learn how to create violence in their communities, etc.

Students also choose to not learn things. Of course, the extreme in this is choosing to leave school rather than continue to face the day-to-day indignities heaped upon them. The paradox is that the student, in doing so, is harming herself or himself—and his or her community—in the process. Recognize that some would argue that this is less an instance of students choosing to drop out and more an instance of students being pushed out; after all, it is not the students' fault that the school is violating their integrity.

Despite what nondominant culture students may be experiencing in the everyday, many develop resilience that allows them to continue forward. Sometimes they even recognize that their very presence and success in school is a form of resistance to oppression.[9]

These students are usually driven and motivated by something much larger than themselves. This inspiring force could be the desire to be role models for their siblings or to honor the sacrifices their parents have made just to assure that they can attend school. It could be the motivation to be successful and return to the local community to serve that community. It could be recognition that they wish to give back to others as a testimony to all the ways in which they have been supported. Whatever the reason, the very presence and resilience students exhibit is, indeed, a form of resistance to prevailing social and school inequalities.

* * *

The United States has a long, painful yet complicated history of race relations and racial tension, bias and discrimination, and status inequalities and social privileges. At the beginning, these were more deliberately set forth in an effort to create a distinctly stratified society based on race, class, gender, disability, sexual orientation, etc. As much as we might wish to forget this history, it is our legacy. But it need not be our trajectory, the future course of the nation.

Contemporarily, we still battle these demons. The racism, sexism, homophobia, etc. of the past has changed with the times, but it is still evident to those who are vigilant of the many new, but subtle, ways in which it presents itself. It has a chameleon-like nature. It includes not only those ways we continue to oppress others based on certain social identity affiliations, but also the ways in which we maintain social privileges for people from other social identity groups.

Luckily, many examples of anti-racist work in schools and communities can be found. We would do well to consider who did this work, what challenges they confronted, how they overcame these challenges, and what sustained them in this work. We would benefit knowing what alliances they created and how those alliances worked.

To those who are socially aware, the walls of the house of multicultural education do tell a story of oppression and resistance. And this story can inform us of the kinds of critical, civic engagement that can advance our nation forward toward a more perfect union.

NOTES

1. Holthouse, 2009.
2. Kohl, 1994.
3. For a description of these, including those listed here, see Nieto & Bode, 2008.
4. Cline, Necochea, & Rios, 2004.
5. See, for example, Myers & Williamson, 2002.
6. Zamudio & Rios, 2006.
7. Nathan, 2005.
8. Given its intersection with ableism, or the discrimination against persons with disabilities, we do not condone the popular usage of "colorblindness" within the field of education, specifically. That said, the term highlights a purposeful ignoring or dissolving of color that cannot be fully captured through alternative terms (i.e., "color neutral"). See Pearson, 2010 for more on this issue.
9. Solórzano & Delgado-Bernal, 2001.

Chapter 5

Room for Living

Multicultural Education through Conversation, Connection, and Collaboration

The heart of our homes—our living room—pulses regularly and rhythmically with the conversations of our friends, family members, and professional acquaintances. In the multicultural education house, this *room for living* is the place where educators meet to collaborate with colleagues and community members in order to transform the theoretical principles of multicultural education into practical applications for specific classrooms, content areas, and students.

Unfortunately, efforts to shift the theory of multicultural education into classroom practice often fall short. In some cases, professional development support may be lacking.[1] Sometimes those involved in the process may not clearly understand the implications for effective multicultural education, so individual efforts fade as time progresses. Educators may resist integrating culture into their classes because they fear they will offend students or encourage increased tension between cultural groups.[2] In order to address the potential hurdles and move a school, district, and community toward sustainable change that supports multicultural education, three Cs—Conversation, Connection, and Collaboration—must play an essential role in the transformation.

CONVERSATION: THE COFFEE TABLE BOOK

The living room is the place where we meet with neighbors to visit about our lives, the final score from last night's basketball game, how we'll vote in the next election, the weather, and the quality of the local schools. For multicultural education, the living room is a powerful place for both celebrating the school's diversity and for igniting new conversations about innovative ways to promote education for cultural responsiveness. In terms of those individuals who are not familiar with the theory and reality of diversity in schools, multicultural education may be like an intriguing and unusual coffee table book.

Some people may ignore the book altogether, noting their already crammed daily schedules: "I'd love to look through that book, but I can barely even get through the work I have to do. . . ." These people view "adding" multicultural education to their plate as impossible and impractical.

When other individuals notice the coffee table book, they may flip through the pages, glancing at the pictures and captions while they hurriedly gobble their lunch: "Huh. Look at that picture—I wonder where that is taken. . . ." For these people, sustainable change is still not clearly defined. They are interested in the concepts and theories of multicultural education, but they do not know where to begin in terms of actual implementation.

Still others may take a few moments to look through the coffee table book, carefully considering the whole picture and the implications for their own lives: "What a beautiful sunset . . . I should take my family for a walk in the park this weekend to watch the sun set." These people are inspired by ideas from within multicultural education theory, and they are spurred into action. In addition, these individuals motivate others to implement new approaches through collaboration, effective leadership, and peer mentorship. The conversations they ignite are filled with exciting possibilities.

Surprisingly, the day-to-day world of education encourages relatively few conversations regarding these innovative practices for educating children. Teaching has historically been an isolated profession that encourages little collaboration between educators and other educational stakeholders.[3] This professional seclusion is detrimental to both teachers and students, as it perpetuates a "self-defeating nature" that discourages growth, preserves power relations within the school structure, and limits sharing of ideas and experiences that can promote multicultural education.[4]

Teachers are not the only ones excluded from the professional conversation in today's schools. Parents, while interested and supportive of their students' education, are often unable to dialogue frequently with educators. Educators may mistake this noninvolvement for a lack of interest, but that is often an inaccurate perspective. Some parents feel uncomfortable in school settings due to language differences, variations in cultural norms, or their own past experiences with education.[5] For example, American Indian parents who attended assimilative boarding schools may hesitate to attend parent-teacher conferences. Immigrant or refugee parents may be reluctant to visit with a teacher because they believe they do not comprehend enough English—the language of power and communication in most schools—to effectively contribute to the dialogue.

It is important to assure that efforts to include those who have been historically excluded from the conversation are successful. For example, simply asking a group of community members for feedback during a whole group discussion will likely encourage responses from only the most outspoken members of the audience. The individuals who are reluctant to participate in a whole group setting may be the ones who can provide truly innovative ideas. Incorporating a variety of formats, from small discussion groups or table murals (large pieces of paper placed on cafeteria tables with markers) to anonymous surveys or idea boxes, into a give-and-take dialogue process can better promote the conversation for all those involved.

It is also critical to discuss the community's expectations with a few respected leaders, in order to consider the potential influence of cultural norms. For example, in some cultures, women are expected to listen when in a large group of men and women. If the school leaders are interested in learning about the ideas of the women, smaller groups or interviews might be more appropriate than whole-group discussions.

Initiating the Conversation

The formation of a team may prove to be an effective initial step when working to advance multicultural education. It is important to include the voices of respected teachers, administrators, parents, community members, cultural leaders, and students who represent a variety of cultural backgrounds as part of this team. The team members should be prepared to openly explore power differences—real or perceived—that may affect efforts to advance multicultural education. Without this critical and reflective dialogue, the amount and type of input may fluctuate from member to member due to variations in cultural expectations and/or familiarity with the field of education. Together, team members can then work to gather information, learn about approaches that may work in your school, connect to the community, and collaborate with a range of educational stakeholders.

Research in Multicultural Contexts

While the use of observation to identify current and best practices in the school might seem like a logical way to begin investigating multicultural education, the concept of "research" holds potentially negative connotations for members of the community. For some cultures, research is equated with oppression, since many researchers have reduced people, cultures, and results to numbers, and those numbers have justified oppressive and discriminatory practices. In the same way that many homeowners would feel uncomfortable during an afternoon conversation with neighbors if a government representative showed up to silently observe and take notes, educational research conducted by outsiders can be intimidating, inappropriate, and even counterproductive. When preparing to conduct any observations or research in schools, consider the following guidelines:

- Become familiar with research in the community—who conducts it, what are the historical implications, and how do the community cultural leaders feel about it?
- Show respect for the stories of community members through inclusion of multiple research formats (i.e., classroom observations, interviews, student focus groups)
- Explain the purpose of observations to students, parents, and teachers
- Allow multiple opportunities for individuals to obtain additional information
- Have people familiar with the school and/or community be those who observe/interview (such as school faculty/staff and community members)
- Encourage observers to spend several days in the classroom prior to formal observations
- Supplement observation with alternative methods to gather information (i.e., use video or audio recordings, anonymous suggestion boxes, etc.)

Learning about Multicultural Education in Your School

Initial conversations should strive to identify past and present practices in terms of school organization, curriculum, instruction, and assessment. How is your school organized physically and structurally? What content knowledge is included in the curriculum, and why? How do educators present information and guide learning? Are current assessment approaches accurately and responsively measuring student learning? How have teachers historically supported multicultural education? What practices has the school abandoned, and why?

In addition to identifying the past and present practices in your school, you might seek to learn about multicultural education efforts that have worked or are working in your community and/or in other communities. While there are no sure-fire, one-sized-fits-all approaches to multicultural education, many experts in the field agree that there are common values. In addition, some general approaches may be applicable in your context, and these ideas may provide guidance for your future efforts. It is important to work closely with community members to determine the appropriateness of these broader approaches within the context of your specific school.

School Organization

When considering this broader scope of multicultural education, one conversational launching point is to consider the influence of school organization on teaching and learning. How do schools that value multicultural learning differ, physically and structurally, from traditional American educational institutions? How are schools traditionally organized, and how does the focus school compare?

You can begin thinking about school organization by mapping the physical spaces of your school. The use of drawings, videotaping, or photography can supplement observations and comments. Regardless of the approach, it is important to map a variety of classrooms and to interview teachers and several students to assure that your perception is representative. Additionally, spaces beyond the classroom should also be mapped, including hallways, cafeterias, computer labs, libraries, gyms, and other common areas.

In addition to mapping physical spaces, you might note other structural aspects of the school. One of the greatest structural hurdles inhibiting the success of multicultural education involves tracking and course selection in schools.[6] For many students, such tracking begins with ability grouping in elementary schools. Once nondominant culture students reach high school, they are significantly under-represented in many advanced courses. These students are often over-represented in remedial courses and special education programs, where they have a much higher rate of having been inaccurately labeled. Such courses tend to focus primarily on test preparation and drills, instead of encouraging the in-depth critical and creative thinking that is often promoted in advanced courses.

For students who may struggle with dominant educational systems, these courses are frustrating ("*another* period of math . . .") and dehumanizing ("I'm in the dummy class"), especially if the students are forced to take them. In contrast, students who are able to participate in selecting their courses have higher levels of confidence and achievement than those simply assigned to courses.[7]

When considering these organizational aspects, you may want to ask: What types of classes are students taking? Are students able to select their own courses? Are students from different backgrounds appropriately represented in advanced courses? How are students grouped? How do students, teachers, and parents feel about these aspects?

You might also want to identify perceived organizational problems through interviews with teachers, students, and parents. All concerns should be

Table 5.1   Organizing Learning Environments to Advance Multicultural Education

Values	Example Introductory Practices
Collaboration is valued	• Classroom layout promotes collaboration (e.g., pods of desks) • Community members guide learning (e.g., students engage in Native water resource management through field science with elders)
Multiculturalism is visible	• Students see themselves represented in the school (e.g., halls contain murals of leaders from various backgrounds, displays include diverse products from many different students) • Students learn about cultural connections to place (e.g., Doc Your Block projects describe local interests) • Structure supports project-based learning, field experiences, and multi-age, multi-ability and/or interdisciplinary learning (e.g., Block periods, school-wide social justice themes)
Diversity is pervasive	• Movement and body language is respectful of cultural norms (e.g., teachers adhere to personal space expectations as defined by specific cultural groups, families, and students) • Students share their unique funds of knowledge (e.g., digital stories share student backgrounds)

valued, even if they do not seem to be immediately linked to multicultural education. For example, a teacher's assertion that "I don't have enough time to plan for my classes" may, on the surface, seem like an organizational issue that is only impacting one teacher's job satisfaction. However, from a multicultural education perspective, this concern could be viewed as a lack of opportunity to learn about and connect to student culture.

After learning about the organizational and structural aspects of your school, you might research practices that could promote multicultural education in and beyond the school. While these practices will vary from school to school due to specific cultural expectations, there are general values that should be considered when organizing for multicultural education (see Table 5.1). The examples we include in this table are only small slices of the larger pie: Critical multicultural education does not utilize these ideas in isolation, but instead weaves together many elements throughout all aspects of education.

Curriculum

Cultural elders are the first educators to teach children, so it is important to consider the norms promoted by the school within the context of the community. Since community and school values frequently conflict for students from diverse backgrounds, children may receive mixed signals regarding the importance of culture in schools.[8] Since curricular design, by definition, "leads to an identifiable program of knowledge and skills to be learned," it inherently promotes a singular perspective.[9] So it potentially conflicts with the tenets of multicultural education.

Multicultural curriculum, in contrast, is innovative and dynamic, which may make it seem difficult to identify and implement. In order to deter marginalization, the curriculum should *integrate* multicultural experiences, instead of following an additive approach. That is, multicultural educators should reject materials that separate cultural information from the "main" or "regular" content (i.e., an isolated chapter on African American literature in an American literature textbook). Materials should appeal to various learning modalities (i.e., look for visuals within the text, supplemental video and audio recordings, planning tips for teachers in terms of ways to make learning active and experiential) to promote multi-faceted learning, which enhances culturally responsive education and reinforces learning for all students.[10]

Multicultural curriculum encompasses a variety of perspectives, honors the narrative experiences of diverse peoples, and connects content to student knowledge in order to promote meaningful learning. Educators and schools that standardize curriculum for all students are not, as they might perceive, promoting equality in the classroom. Standardized curriculum often serves as a means to sort students and it tends to recognize diversity as a deficit rather than strength. Furthermore, a standardized curriculum that reinforces traditional content and epistemologies alone dismisses or only superficially includes diverse perspectives and sends an ethnocentric message: Even though you are different, you should only learn about this content, because it is the "best."[11]

In order to evaluate the quality of the curriculum, you can ask a variety of questions. What programs and textbooks are used, and why were they selected? Where were they created or published, and for what audience? Who was involved in the process of development? What research has been done regarding the curriculum materials, both in and beyond the district? How do teachers, students, parents, and others feel about the curriculum?

Following this step, you might look more specifically at the voices and ideas that are supported through the curriculum (see Table 5.2). With respect to Language Arts, for example, are writers from various cultural backgrounds equally represented? In terms of Math, does the text provide various visual models in addition to linear, text-based explanations? Are nondominant culture experiences integrated into the curriculum, or simply added as an afterthought in a text box or special section/chapter in the history texts?

Table 5.2   Developing Curriculum to Advance Multicultural Education

Values	Example Introductory Practices
Diverse views are integrated into the content	• Textbooks integrate multiple perspectives • Images accurately represent people from various backgrounds • Students analyze curriculum
Many voices contribute to the dialogue	• Resources contain perspectives of people from various cultural backgrounds • Authors are members of the described cultural group
Various formats guide learning	• Resources include a variety of activities and assessments
Cultural beliefs are preserved and perpetuated	• Explanations of ceremonies and traditions are respectful and preserve cultural norms
Knowledge is dynamic	• Curriculum extends beyond the "canon" of knowledge • Students and teachers supplement the curriculum with culturally relevant, community-centered resources
Learning connects to relevant topics	• Students can explain how the content connects to their lives • Curriculum encourages community-centered learning

Instruction

Instruction is one of the most powerful components of education in today's schools, since teachers who are able to develop caring relationships with their students through instruction not only improve achievement, but also boost resiliency.[12] The idea, as explained by Pang (2005), is that "conditions of caring, community, and culture in classrooms produce higher levels of achievement that lead to greater social efficacy. This more effective learning community empowers and prepares all students to work toward social, political, and economic justice" (p. 217). With this in mind, you might choose to review current instructional practices in your school, as well as the practices of educators in other schools that have developed a reputation for advancing multicultural education. In addition to classroom observations, you should discuss instruction with teachers, instructional facilitators, and other instructional leaders. It is important to gather comprehensive information, so observations and interviews should take place regularly over the course of several months.

There are several key questions to consider when observing instruction. Who is talking in class (student time vs. teacher time)? Are students all actively involved in learning? Are they building on previous learning? Do all students have opportunities to contribute and connect the learning to their prior understanding? Most importantly, does the teacher promote a caring learning environment that encourages students to take pride in their unique identities?

Culturally responsive instruction centers on the learner's construction of meaning, rather than the content or the teacher's own knowledge or experience. Multicultural classrooms utilize more innovative instructional strategies, such as hands-on and collaborative learning, than "traditional" learning environments, which tend to favor teacher-centered approaches such as direct instruction and presentation.[13] Most importantly, responsive instructors respond to the unique needs of their students with a variety of approaches each class period.

A potential obstacle to both culturally responsive instruction and multicultural curriculum is the classroom teacher. For veteran teachers, it can be difficult to give up a lesson that has previously ignited enthusiasm among students, but, for various reasons, is not resonating with today's learners. Teachers are often concerned they will offend a student, so they may further limit culturally responsive teaching in their own classrooms. Sometimes this reluctance is also due to the fact that many teachers are confronted with molding instruction for more than one or two different cultural groups. This task can seem daunting or impossible.

As we have emphasized in earlier chapters, it is important to note that there is no single, best approach for teaching groups of students. In other words, there is no standard "African American educational model" or "Latina/o curriculum." However, students from diverse cultural backgrounds may benefit from similar instructional practices.[14] Teachers may not need to create 27 different lesson plans, but they do need to integrate all of the values that guide culturally responsive instruction (see Table 5.3).

Table 5.3 Developing Instruction to Advance Multicultural Education

Values	*Example Introductory Practices*
Diverse view are valued throughout the instructional process	• Teachers use multiple instructional strategies (e.g.- collaborative learning, problem-based learning, discussion) throughout each lesson • Students have opportunities to share ideas and experiences • The teacher does not monopolize discussions
Learning is dynamic and constructed through experience	• Students connect to prior experiences • Students participate in hands-on, community based learning (e.g.- students interview community elders, then share the stories with classmates)
People are respected as individuals and as group members	• Teachers provide daily opportunities for students to explore their individual and cultural identities • Students are not asked to "represent" their culture

Assessment

Assessment is a powerful and influential force in today's schools. While over-assessing students can impede learning, well-constructed, culturally responsive assessments can provide teachers, parents, schools, and communities—as well as the students themselves—with valuable information regarding curriculum appropriateness, instructional effectiveness, and skill attainment—all of which can promote multicultural education.

It is important to understand that assessments come in a variety of formats, from individually completed traditional paper and pencil objective tests to cooperative community-based projects. The type and composition of assessments used are indicative of district priorities, including how the district defines important knowledge. Many school tests focus on a relatively narrow and static body of information and skills, despite our dynamic population, changing technology use, and growing amount of accessible knowledge.[15]

When considering the role of assessment in your school, look for certain assessment characteristics (see Table 5.4). Learn about the required assessments in your school and district. What are they, what do they test, who created them, how long have they been used, and how do teachers, parents, and students feel about their overall effectiveness in terms of testing what they claim to test?

Table 5.4 Developing Assessments to Advance Multicultural Education

Values	Example Introductory Practices
Learning can be measured in many different ways	• Traditional tests comprise only one component of assessment • Students are able to share their learning through art, music, collaborative projects, etc.
Learning is contextual and culture-dependent	• Students are able to demonstrate understanding through real-world applications • Learning is shared with audiences of community members • Tests are free of cultural bias and stereotypes • Assessments include experiences that all students can recognize and understand
Understanding is defined by cultural groups	• Students are tested on the subject and skills and are not put in a double-jeopardy situation (e.g., students who cannot read at grade level but who excel in science are not punished with a science test that requires extensive reading) • Teachers work with parents and community members to monitor their students' learning and re-teach as needed • Assessments are not randomly plugged into the school year

Another key consideration is the type of assessments. Are most of the assessments primarily written tests, or are there a variety of types? Are projects, performance, and cooperative assessments used? For classrooms that enhance learning for diverse students, as well as those that truly challenge students who learn in more traditional ways, it is essential to include a range of assessment types.

Culturally responsive assessments accurately measure what they are intended to measure. This becomes complicated if you consider the fact that, even outside of language arts, students are traditionally assessed through reading and writing skills. For example, even though a student may understand science, if he/she struggles with reading or is still learning English, success on a test might be impossible if the student is required to read a passage based on material learned during science class. The obstacle created by the reading difficulty does not accurately evaluate this student's understanding of science concepts in this case.

In addition to providing an accurate measurement, assessments should be meaningful to teachers, students, and parents. Authentic assessments such as projects, presentations, and portfolios can help students develop life-long skills. Community-based assessments, such as cataloguing historical letters or testing local water quality, become even more meaningful if students are able to share their learning with parents, elders, and neighbors. This experiential assessment is powerful for all students, and it provides a format to empower students from nondominant cultural backgrounds within their schools and communities.

Finally, culturally responsive assessments should be free of bias. This is the most challenging aspect of assessment, but it is essential. Sometimes, bias is obvious ("Columbus discovered America in what year?"), but more often it is subtle. For example, students who have never been to rural areas may not be able to select synonyms based on farm buildings ("silo" is to "storage unit"). Regardless of the severity or level of awareness, bias is unacceptable in a school that is striving to advance multicultural education.

CONNECTION: INVITING THE COMMUNITY INTO YOUR LIVING ROOM

Although people may be strangers when they are initially invited into the living room, they often leave as friends. Communities and connections are created and strengthened in living rooms, since they serve as a bridge between our private and public lives. Following the initial conversations about multicultural education, local cultural leaders should be invited into the living room to share their experiences and ideas.

This building phase hinges upon actively seeking out new perspectives. Usually, these perspectives are those previously underrepresented in the schools: They are the voices of nondominant cultural group members within and beyond the community. For many cultural groups, asking for the advice of others within the community is not only appreciated, it is expected—especially when it comes to issues related to the education of young people.[16]

The first step in developing a working relationship with community members is to increase educator involvement in the community. Providing incentives and support for teachers and other school staff to attend community events, to volunteer outside of school settings, or to expand service learning opportunities are all possible ways to increase educator participation in the community.

This involvement can be enhanced through experiential or community-based instruction. For students and teachers, learning in the community (learning in context) can be very powerful, since it validates cultural identity, instills a sense of pride in self and community, and fosters relationships between the school and family.[17] For parents who are not comfortable in school settings, this type of learning provides an opportunity for non-threatening involvement in education. Teachers can invite parents to lead field experiences or demonstrate real world applications for skills introduced in the classroom.

Second, collaboration with community members should affect professional development for teachers. Some school officials feel compelled to seek external experts to facilitate professional development, potentially spending thousands of dollars each year to cover consultant expenses and workshop fees. Combined with the limited support and follow up after the professional development that frequently accompanies workshops conducted by outsiders, resistance from the community and teachers may spell disaster for such initiatives.[18] Therefore, it is important to investigate as many options as possible. Are there local solutions available? Culturally responsive professional development should involve local resources and regular, continuing staff training.[19]

Additionally, schools should strive to develop partnerships with the community. From inviting community leaders and elders to school board meetings to the creation of a grandparent program where community elders assist teachers in the classroom, there are many opportunities for strengthened community involvement. In some communities, a family feast is a more appropriate alternative to the traditional, and often intimidating, parent-teacher conference. Again, seeking input from leaders within the community is the best starting point.

If the community is not very diverse, there are still opportunities to establish connections with cultural experts who can help guide the process and contribute to the conversations regarding multicultural education in the school. Seeking out leaders in neighboring communities or creating a partnership with multicultural organizations (see Chapter 8 for more information on this) are possible ways to connect the community with various cultural groups. It is important to recognize that experiential learning is valuable for educators and community members as well as the students in the schools. When possible, it is essential to avoid contrived situations. Instead, strive to create meaningful multicultural connections for those in the community and school.

COLLABORATION: LEAVING THE COUCH

Of course, growing overly comfortable in the living room can promote inaction. A common problem in terms of school reform is that educators and educational stakeholders turn into multicultural education couch potatoes—they are eager to listen to the ideas of community members, but they are resistant in terms of actual implementation. Once you have identified the current models being used and potential ways to enhance multicultural education in your schools, the action phase must begin. For many school districts, this is the phase that is, unfortunately, the most neglected. It is, in fact, the most critical stage of the process.

In general, collaboration should lead to practical outcomes as co-developed by educators and community members. Careful steps must be taken to assure that collaboration does not result in dominant culture leadership defining the agenda, while nondominant culture participants are ignored or included as token members of the cultural community. While it is important to have concrete ideas in mind in terms of the direction of the collaboration before beginning the process, it is also important to ensure that pursuing such concrete or practical ideas does not privilege dominant culture approaches and measures while silencing community member input. To encourage change on school and classroom levels, educators and administrators must also have a collaborative voice in the process. Planning should not undermine the professionalism of teachers, so it is essential to include them in all aspects.[20]

Professional development also needs to be structured to promote positive change that best supports socially just and culturally responsive teaching. Professional Learning Communities (PLCs), Lesson Study models, and other collaborative approaches can facilitate responsive growth without belittling teachers and their professional experience.[21] Educational innovation requires much more than implementation of mandated programs or modes of instructional delivery; it should encourage a shift in attitudes about teaching and learning.[22] Collaboration promotes a sense of professional pride among teachers and community members, and it provides a format for learning about education for social justice by recognizing those individuals frequently silenced in terms of educational policy reform.

For both community members and educators, practicality is often at the center of educational reform, but such practicality is heavily contextual: It depends on the unique characteristics of the school and community. Therefore, evidence to support change should be specific in terms of your community and school. In other words, it is more effective and powerful to introduce collaborative reform efforts through the voices of local teachers, parents, and students than to discuss nationwide statistics or rely exclusively on external consultants.[23] Since education for social justice hinges on shifting perceptions regarding the historical view of schools, providing professional development opportunities that are specific and practical, as collaboratively and responsively determined, can help support all those involved in the mutual adaptation that is vital for successful transformation.[24]

The collaborative process should address a timely need as well. In other words, if teachers believe that there is something more pressing to consider, they may not be as supportive of the collaborative process, of multicultural education, or of the implementation of strategies.[25] Today's educators experience increased work expectations, which erode the privileges and professionalism of teachers.[26] Co-developing goals with educators and community members early in the process can help support teacher and community buy in.

Creating Goals for Educators

For many schools in today's climate of standards-based curriculum, instruction, and assessment, it can be very challenging to recognize opportunities for advancing multicultural education. Teachers may feel that they are being asked to add something else to their already crowded plate, or they may feel ill prepared to implement culturally responsive instruction.[27]

To further complicate matters, collaboration can increase frustration for educators and community members, due to differences in communication approaches and ways of knowing. Dominant culture teachers, for example, may want clear-cut examples of responsive practices for implementation, while community members may feel uncomfortable defining responsive practices in static and potentially narrow terms.

Table 5.5 MAPS Model for Developing Goals and Practices to Advance Multicultural Education

Guideline	Ineffective	Effective
Measurable	The school library will increase its selection of multicultural books and resources.	The school library will obtain 100 new multicultural titles.
Achievable	Students will gain proficiency of a second language.	Students will deliver a presentation demonstrating conversational second language proficiency to a panel of community members who speak the language.
Practical	Students will compare/contrast traditions of African cultures.	Students will compare/contrast traditions of African cultures and connect their findings to their own experiences.
Specific	The student body will become more aware of multiculturalism.	All students will be able to identify the five values of multiculturalism as defined by the tribal Council of Elders.

Although responsive collaborative processes should draw first upon community funds of knowledge, it is important to guide educators and educational stakeholders through the process of seeing *how* to make the changes that are suggested. It may be helpful to utilize the MAPS approach to facilitate implementation (see Table 5.5), although it is important to note that nondominant culture groups may or may not value these guidelines to the extent that dominant culture members might. In your work with community members, you may identify different guidelines that more appropriately fit the needs of your community and school.

Identifying practices and goals that are *measurable* may help educators who are unfamiliar with multicultural education and overwhelmed by the day-to-day demands of teaching. When teachers are not able to clearly identify the results of their efforts, they are less likely to continue those efforts. Selecting practices and goals with clear results can encourage educators to continue learning and changing. Not only should goals be measurable, but the measure itself should also be culturally responsive and co-developed by the teachers and community members themselves when possible.

Second, implementing *achievable* practices may allow such educators to track their own development and provide an incentive to commit to change. Even if the goal is a long-term one, there should be short-term benchmarks to demonstrate that progress is occurring. When considering whether or not a goal or practice is achievable, it is important for educators and educational stakeholders to consult with cultural leaders and other community members in order to avoid selecting approaches that are based on deficit views of diverse learners.

Third, goals and practices should be *practical* as determined by both community members and educators. Again, many schools today are faced with a plethora of programs and quick fixes. Program goals should be challenging and relevant for the community and students. Since teachers may perceive themselves as being objective professionals acting in the best interests of children, a practical, experiential approach to professional development may be the best format for encouraging educators, and others, to shift their thinking about multicultural education.[28] Travel opportunities to schools that have implemented multicultural education can also help teachers expand their awareness and recognize the practicality of strategies.[29]

Finally, goals and practices should be defined in *specific* terms that are appropriate for students, parents, and teachers. As is true for all aspects of the collaborative process, these terms should be determined by educators *and* community members. If they are not collaboratively developed, there is a potential for dominant culture participants to water down the complexity of concepts due to a deficit view of the community.

MAKING THE HOUSE OF MULTICULTURAL EDUCATION YOUR HOME

The most important consideration in terms of advancing multicultural education is to make it clear to all participants and community members that the process will be a sustainable effort. Making a house a home requires commitment and risk taking. It is not sufficient to simply lay out a doormat that announces "Welcome to Our Home"—a home cannot be made with an isolated event, by a single individual, or with a gimmick. Instead, building a home demands a connection of practices and habits, many people, and real experiences. Similarly, advancing multicultural education requires a connection of and commitment to each and every one of the general, introductory values described in this chapter. It requires the engaged, collaborative participation of many people—teachers, administrators, support faculty and staff, as well as community members, cultural leaders, and students. It is not something that can be checked off a list or addressed exclusively with a gimmick or program.

Therefore, if culturally responsive education is important to your school, it is essential that time is provided to allow faculty and staff to regularly revisit the focus, discover successes and challenges, and continue to develop practical ideas collaboratively. The presentation of a one-shot workshop sends a message that the extended journey is not worthwhile.

In addition to the formal workshop sessions, effective collaboration requires consistent informal support. One of the best ways to increase teacher success with new approaches is to increase structured, collaborative planning time. In addition (not as a substitute) to their current planning time, teachers should be given time to work with mentors, instructional and cultural facilitators, community members, and other colleagues. Students should be included in the collaborative process as well.

Schools that support interdisciplinary, thematic experiences encourage students to investigate topics at critical levels. Culturally responsive schools, since they promote connections between school and home, discourage the fragmentation of learning that often comes with isolated subjects ("first I have math, then I go to PE, then I have . . .") or standardized curriculum programs that are disconnected from the other subjects offered in the school. Additional practices that show promise for advancing teacher-student and collaboration include teacher looping (teachers stay with the same group of students for several years), home room programs that promote team-building and community involvement, and alternative school times (such as late starts or evening classes).

Community members should play central roles in the collaborative process. In addition to involvement with professional development, community members should be involved in classroom settings as often as possible. Some schools, for example, have highly effective grandparent programs, where elders support teachers in the classroom. Inviting community members into the classroom for guest presentations can be very important as well. Teachers should think outside of the box, and the traditional classroom, to connect the school to the community. Organizing field-based learning at local sites can be extremely powerful for students, teachers, and community members.

It is important to note that the practices outlined in this chapter only represent a starting point. We hope you will strive to implement these ideas holistically and often, rather than in isolation or infrequently. Most importantly, we hope that you will look beyond these introductory ideas in order to turn the house of multicultural education into your home. See Chapter 7 for more ideas regarding ways to advance *critical* multicultural education.

* * *

Like the living room in our homes, multicultural education can provide a place to encourage innovative dialogue, foster new relationships, and initiate action and change. In terms of educational reform, the life stories of key individuals—teachers, parents, community members, cultural leaders, and students—are often ignored. Through conversations, community connections, and collaboration, schools can open the door to the house of multicultural education. Together, we can make the house of multicultural education our home.

NOTES

1. See, for example, Wallin McLaughlin, 1976, and Zmuda, Kuklis, & Kline, 2004.
2. Nieto & Bode, 2008 describe this concern, and offer ideas for teachers.
3. Zmuda, Kuklis, & Kline, 2004, p. 9.
4. See, for example, Silin, 1995, p. 237, and, Eisner, 2004, p. 300.
5. Nieto & Bode, 2008.
6. Although many researchers began observing the negative impacts of tracking decades ago, the problems continue. See Ladson-Billings & Tate, 1995; Noddings, 2004; and, Rose, 1989.
7. See reports on block scheduling and student engagement, such as U.S. Department of Education, 2003.
8. Garcia & Guerra, 2006.
9. Hlebowitsh, 2004.
10. Brain research suggests that multimodal instruction supports deeper learning and responsive education. See Anderson, 1997 and American Association of University Women, 1992.
11. Noddings, 2004, p. 336.
12. Extensive research identifies several elements that support culturally responsive instruction. See Marzano, Pickering, & Pollock, 2001, and Waxman, Padron, & Gray, 2003.
13. Sleeter & Grant, 2009.
14. Gay, 2003/2004.
15. Kornhaber, 2004.
16. Hidalgo, Siu, & Epstein, 2004.
17. Moll & Gonzalez, 2004.
18. Nieto & Bode, 2008, and Zmuda Kuklis, & Kline, 2004.
19. See, for example Wallin McLaughlin, 1976, The Center for Black Literature, and the Center for Law and Social Policy.
20. Considerable information exists regarding the unique learning needs of adult learners. See, for example, Fogarty & Pete, 2004, and Zmuda, Kuklis, & Kline, 2004.
21. Professional Learning Communities (PLCs) and Lesson Study models utilize collaborative learning at the professional level to emphasize teamwork, respect, growth, and peer coaching, as opposed to hierarchical evaluation of teaching. For

more regarding PLCs, see Dufour & Eaker, 1998. For more regarding Lesson Study, see Fernandez, Cannon, & Chokshi, 2003.

22. Wallin McLaughlin, 1976.
23. Wallin McLaughlin, 1976.
24. Wallin McLaughlin, 1976.
25. Zmuda, Kuklis, & Kline, 2004.
26. Apple, 1986.
27. Gay, 2000.
28. Silin, 2004; Wallin McLaughlin, 1976.
29. Wallin McLaughlin, 1976.

Chapter 6

The Kitchen

The Myths and Misconceptions of Multicultural Education

Given the many important reasons for multicultural education, you may wonder why anyone resists responsive practices, especially if practical ideas have been shared and learned. Stakeholders and teachers may believe that certain content, reflective of the dominant culture, is more valuable than multicultural content. People (students included) may expect multicultural education to result in lower expectations than more rigorous (i.e., traditional) approaches to education. Sometimes, our schools themselves interfere with responsive practice due to physical layout, approaches to scheduling, and sorting of students into advanced or remedial tracks. Some educational stakeholders and teachers may believe that separate approaches to education, such as tracking, are acceptable as a means to promote skill attainment and justice.

As humans, we often form our understanding as a result of both experience and second-hand information. In some cases, the second-hand information we receive is based in the real experiences of others, but many times that information is the result of shaded reality, blurred rememberings, or myth. Some myths, like the story of the monster 50-pound fish that my uncle supposedly caught in an irrigation ditch, are clearly exaggerated. Others, like the myth of Columbus' peaceful landing in the Americas, may be more difficult to recognize as mistruths. Those myths are generally accepted by mainstream culture, despite the opposing facts.

Such myths are also passed from one generation to another, and from teacher to student. As a result, generations of young people grow up believing such falsehoods. Students believe Columbus "discovered" the present-day mainland United States, that his treatment of the Indigenous peoples he encountered was positive and welcomed, and that his accomplishment signaled the dawn of a wonderful nation.

83

In reality, Columbus never landed on the mainland of what is now the United States, he enslaved and supported the rape and abuse of the Taino people, and his accomplishments opened the door to mass oppression, genocide, and slavery throughout the Western Hemisphere. When such a myth persists across decades—in this case, centuries—educational, political, and social injustice continues. In the context of today's schools, such myths influence teaching and people's lives in very real ways.

Like a kitchen where food—and story—is "cooked up," the kitchen in the house of multicultural education is the place where myth and reality blur. However, the kitchen is also home to the kitchen table, where honest and provocative conversations occur. This chapter puts the myths and misconceptions that surround the field of multicultural education on the table for discussion. Like many myths that affect our understanding, these myths often have connections to real events or concerns. Only after we seek to understand those connections can we recognize the myths for what they are—products of tradition, fear, naïveté, and misunderstanding.

MYTH #1: MULTICULTURAL EDUCATION SEEKS TO REPLACE CORE AMERICAN KNOWLEDGE.

Background of the Myth

As educators, parents, and community members, we strive to provide our children with the best access to learning. We want our students to be prepared to succeed in the workplace, in higher education, or in whatever professional and personal activities they choose to pursue. When it comes to the education of our young people, we are often reluctant to change things too quickly because too much is at stake. We wonder: "If it ain't broke, why fix it?"

This perspective is closely tied to one of the central myths that influences—or destroys—the potential for multicultural education in today's schools. Those who are skeptical of multicultural education often raise concerns about the importance of common "cultural" knowledge. For example, E.D. Hirsch (1987) advocates for a "cultural literacy" for all students in the United States. Such cultural literacy centers upon a body of knowledge that Hirsch believes connects and defines us as Americans. In many ways, Hirsch's argument makes sense. If Americans all speak the same language (English) and understand the same core ideas and values (those defined by Hirsch), then we'll all get along, right?

Some of the greatest advocates of Hirsch's perspective are parents. Parents want their children to be prepared to succeed in a world seemingly controlled by specialized academic information. If teachers and schools can help young people acquire a basic understanding of that information—what is termed "cultural capital"[1]—those young people will be better positioned in terms of economic and political success, it seems.

In fact, some of the strongest proponents of a common curriculum and/ or classics-based content are nondominant culture parents themselves, who worry that their children will fall further behind if they are not exposed to cultural capital, such as the cultural literacy Hirsch describes. We have heard parents explain that they want their children to speak only English, or to exclusively read "classic" literature, or to focus more on learning how to take notes during a lecture than how to critique the ideas, because "that is what it takes to do well in school."

Teachers also resist multicultural education based on this myth. Like parents and policy makers, teachers may see the importance in providing students with the cultural capital needed to succeed in dominant culture institutions and settings. In addition, teachers may harbor a bias about specific content, believing that works written by White males truly *are* more valuable than works written by nondominant culture women authors, for example.

To be fair, those teachers may be justified in their views, based upon *their* own understanding of the specific content area. As students and teachers, we may have limited, if any, exposure to non-Western content or the nuances of evaluating that content using nondominant culture perspectives. Our professional identities, as we've always understood them, may be compromised if we suddenly accept that we don't have a complete expertise. Dramatically changing the way we teach and what we teach suggests we are not experts, and it requires support and learning on our part, which can be time-intensive and mentally exhausting. Furthermore, teaching content from a variety of perspectives opens the door to confusion and discomfort, since sometimes the versions of the story conflict. Learning to integrate multicultural education into one's teaching is challenging for teachers, whether they are established veterans or early career educators.

While established teachers may not have much experience with or exposure to multicultural content and approaches, new teachers often encounter basic methods as part of their teacher education program. Despite the support from academia and research entities, the new teachers may find it challenging to implement multicultural education once they begin working in schools. Given the focus on standardized curriculum and test preparation, teachers may believe it is too difficult to carve out the time needed to innovate and implement multicultural education. They may face pressure from some veteran teachers, who frown upon the integration of multicultural education since it signals a change to the way things have been done. Early career teachers, who are often eager to gain the respect of colleagues, parents, and administrators, are especially susceptible to the pressure to fit into the teaching culture.[2]

Students, too, sometimes resist multicultural education. Those who encounter multicultural content may assume they are in "the dummy class" if they are not reading Shakespeare or studying Ancient Greece like their peers. They may worry about their marketability in terms of colleges or universities. They may want to look smart around their friends, so access to the knowledge that is most noticeably valued in the mainstream is important. A final reason, that they are ashamed or embarrassed by multicultural content, is frightening and tied to the persistent tensions that plague society and schools. In these cases, both dominant culture and nondominant culture students may actually believe that multicultural knowledge and diverse ways of knowing are inferior to Eurocentric content and traditional approaches to teaching and assessment.

Challenging the Myth

While these concerns are very real, they are rooted in misunderstanding, fear, compliance, and inaccuracy. When schools give in to the myths, they are left with static, and limited, bodies of information. Although policy makers often point to the concern that the United States is losing competitiveness in the global realm of education, very little has been done in terms of substantial curricular overhaul at any point in the history of public education in the United States. In many ways, students today learn the same material their parents, grandparents, and great-grandparents learned. Furthermore, they learn that material in the same way, and their understanding is measured in the same way. In order to innovate in our schools, we must view education as dynamic and expanding.

It is important to note that multicultural education is inclusive. It is not the intent of multicultural theorists or teachers who utilize multicultural education to replace the literary and artistic works of European and Euro-Americans, to eliminate all references to Western history, or to extinguish the voices of White political figures. Instead, the goal is to *expand* the body of knowledge so that it includes more than a few limited and static pieces of knowledge and viewpoints. Multicultural education offers a multi-faceted view that encourages higher-level critical thinking, awareness of contemporary topics, and effective communication skills to meet the needs of today's diverse and global society.

Instead of focusing exclusively on Western-oriented cultural capital and content, educational stakeholders can advocate for a more expansive and dynamic body of content in their local schools, and on state and federal levels. As members of society, we should also emphasize the importance of shifting from a system that privileges one perspective, to a society that recognizes and values multiple perspectives.

On a practical level, it is important to realize that teachers can incorporate basic multicultural education principles into their classrooms daily, even if there is little flexibility for innovation. Often, curriculum is selected based on its potential to align with national, state, or local standards, so our work on curriculum selection teams is vital. Responsive teachers know that multicultural content aligns well—perhaps better than Eurocentric content—with many of the perspectives that guide much of our educational practice today. Professional organizations, teacher education programs, and national standards boards often emphasize the importance of diversity and critical thinking.

Therefore, the concern about "adding to the curricular plate" does not usually stem from a look at the standards for any particular field or grade level. The main challenges arise when schools have adopted specific curriculum tools that do not already include diverse perspectives. In many cases, understaffed and economically challenged districts make curricular choices based primarily on test data and effective marketing campaigns. Large curriculum publishing companies, which have extensive resources, are better equipped to sell their products to such districts than small companies that may be better able to meet the needs of a specific community. Districts that are committed to multicultural education must look beyond the advertising gimmicks to the quality and diversity of content, the cultural expertise of the publishers and editors, and the contributors' backgrounds.

Even if districts choose less responsive curriculum, teachers should not throw their hands helplessly into the air. If crunched for time, responsive teachers take advantage of transitions, interdisciplinary connections, and creating a visually responsive classroom environment. They also work to inspire and inform curriculum selection teams in order to transform the curriculum the next time textbooks or other curriculum resources are on the discussion table. Furthermore, responsive teachers recognize that multicultural education extends far beyond curriculum. Responsive education includes student-centered instruction and classroom management, as well as diverse, authentic, and holistic views of assessment. See Chapter 5 of this book for a variety of specific ideas for classroom practice.

MYTH #2: MULTICULTURAL EDUCATION IS ABOUT POLITICAL CORRECTNESS INSTEAD OF RIGOR

Background of the Myth

In many ways, society has progressed significantly in terms of multicultural awareness, and many of these gains have been made in only a few decades. One of the reasons such change has occurred so quickly is that legislative mandates and judicial precedents have urged—some suggest forced—reluctant individuals to confront challenges associated with living in a diverse democracy. From affirmative action efforts to sexual discrimination policies in the workplace, these initiatives often have a foundation in justice and multiculturalism, but the way they are implemented sometimes skews the intentions. One of the popular myths surrounding multicultural education focuses on similar concerns: Is multicultural education just another idea rooted in political correctness? Is it more about having nondominant culture students feel good about themselves than it is about having all students learn academic skills?

First, it is important to realize that multicultural education, like many other educational topics, is simultaneously an academic field and a political view. As such, it has the potential to support biased views and varied agendas. Teachers, administrators, and policy makers can work closely with the community to determine expectations and to identify potential areas of bias.

Furthermore, the existing research within the field of multicultural education can offer a guide for individuals striving to incorporate innovative practices in their schools. Even if you are the only proponent of multicultural education in your specific school, you are not alone when you consider the broader scope of educational theory and practice. Research clearly supports connecting content to student experiences and interests, utilizing a variety of approaches to instruction, and encouraging students to demonstrate understanding through application of critical thinking skills.[3] All of these practices align well with multicultural education.

Despite an increasing focus on best practices research that suggests multicultural education is connected to increased achievement for all students, some people may still view efforts to expand multicultural education as tied to political correctness. These individuals may argue that multicultural education is most appropriate in specialized, small group settings or in pull-out environments common to special education, test preparation, and second-language acquisition. In these settings, students from diverse backgrounds are viewed as abnormal or deficient when compared to their White, middle-class peers. Sometimes this perspective results from analysis of test results or for the sake of convenience, while other times the opinion arises from deep-seated prejudice.

As a result of these views, schools may implement multicultural education to provide targeted test preparation or remediation. In many cases, it is difficult to determine which came first, the remedial coursework or the multicultural education. Effective teachers have always tried to connect with their students though the use of relevant content, engaging instructional approaches, and useful assessment tools. If the majority of students in a remedial math course speak Spanish and are immigrants from Mexico, then the teacher may strive to connect some of the math concepts—such as the math developed by the Mayans—to Mexican culture and use some Spanish language to communicate. The ethical and professional challenges arise when the teacher does not do those things at all, no other courses validate Mexican culture, or "Mexican Math" becomes synonymous with "Remedial Math."

Teachers and stakeholders may assert that inclusive, mixed-group settings provide more responsive education than the traditional segregation often seen in remedial and language acquisition courses, since mixed classrooms often do not draw attention to any culture other than "American" culture. On the surface, this sounds like a positive step in terms of respect and democracy, but in reality it too devalues differences and encourages assimilation into one generic culture—the dominant culture. In these classrooms, content focuses on one version of one story, instead of multiple perspectives.

Some teachers, parents, and other stakeholders may worry that schools may actually *perpetuate* injustice for their nondominant culture students through multicultural education. This concern may stem from the view that the education of nondominant culture students should center upon increasing access to mainstream cultural capital, as discussed under Myth #1. In other cases, the view is similar to the one supported by opponents of welfare programs.

If people believe that multicultural education consists of watered down content, enabling instructional approaches, or easy tests, they may believe that schools that utilize multicultural education are actually providing a disservice to both dominant culture and nondominant culture students. This perspective is based upon a misunderstanding of the more critical forms of multicultural education, which rely upon challenging, dynamic content, diverse and multi-modal instructional methods, and a holistic view of rigorous assessment.

Challenging the Myth

When embarking on an effort to expand multicultural education in your school, it is important to have a clear understanding of the different approaches to multicultural education and to go beyond additive "foods and festivals" approaches. Multicultural education should not be something teachers and students *do* once in a while in order to check it off the list.

Multicultural education is about personal and professional transformation, so it should be meaningful, comprehensive, and tied to lifelong learning for both students and educators. To make such learning sustainable, teachers and stakeholders must emphasize the reality that multicultural education is a journey, not a destination or a one-shot experience. Since multicultural education requires a new way of seeing the world for many teachers and students, it is, in many ways, *more* rigorous than previously privileged, traditional approaches to teaching.

In addition to enhancing communication skills and critical thinking, which both contribute to the ability of students to interpret rigorous content, multicultural education improves academic achievement across the board. Research shows that students who are able to see themselves in the curriculum, instruction, and assessment of a particular school do more than develop a stronger sense of self: They perform better on state and national assessments, they are more likely to graduate, they attend and complete college at higher rates, and they engage more effectively in democratic and civic practices.[4]

Finally, multicultural education is not about providing advantages to some students while disadvantaging others. Instead, it is about assuring academic and cultural success for all students. Many teachers and stakeholders believe that the best way to ensure educational justice is to provide exactly the same opportunities to all students. While such an approach supports the concept of educational equality, it does not promote true educational equity.

It is important to recognize that these two concepts—equality and equity—do not have the same meaning in schools today. Equality does not take into consideration differences in background from child to child, the cultural capital that each child brings to school, or the generations of advantages from which certain students' families have benefited. Equity, on the other hand, refers to the recognition that children are not blank slates when they enter a classroom. They come from different backgrounds, have unique experiences, and require different tools to be successful. Equity is about honoring the differences of students and adjusting our teaching practice in order to assure success for all students.

An analogy can help us better understand the difference between equality and equity in learning. Imagine that two teams—one of adolescent girls and the other of adolescent boys—are given equal preparation to play an American football game against each other. They receive the exact same uniforms, coaching, and diet. Of course, the uniforms are created based on decades of male-only football, and the coaching stems from the long tradition of coaching only boys and men in the sport. It is unlikely (though possible) that the girls would win the game in this scenario. In classrooms, it is similarly unlikely that all students will succeed if we use only the traditional materials and methods that have systematically prevented the success of certain students throughout history.

In the football analogy, using traditional equipment and coaching methods does not consider physical or sociological differences between men and women. If we ignore the physical diversity of the players, we cannot control or avoid—at least in the present day—the impact of socialization on potential success. Even with the exact same coaching, the boys might be hesitant to play to their full physical potential, because they may have been socialized to treat women as fragile beings. The girls may not be as aggressive or confident as their male counterparts for the same reason.

As educators, we may (and do) ignore physical and emotional differences in our classrooms. Some educators claim "cultural blindness" and equality for all students, even if those differences mean students come into our classrooms with very different skills, talents, and needs. Ignoring the differences also neglects the reality that outside of our classrooms, students recognize and question diversity due to socialization practices, informal and cultural education, and the media's portrayal of gender, ethnicity, and socioeconomic status.

Some people only see possibilities in shades of either-or. Either the football teams play with equal expectations, preparation, support, and rules, or they don't play each other at all. For many of these individuals, the girls, who may not be prepared to play the game as traditionally defined, should not play football at all. Instead, they should be encouraged to engage in more gender-appropriate activities, such as cheerleading or volleyball. Another option is to place the girls into an all-girls football league. While the cheerleading, volleyball, or the all-girls league may be held to standards that are just as rigorous as the boys', these activities may be viewed as substandard when compared to the boys' sports, thanks to the impact of socialization and the media. In terms of multicultural education, different classes, such as ethnic studies courses, are often viewed this way. Although they may be extremely rigorous, it is difficult to overcome a mindset that is tied to tradition or public opinion.

Beyond the either-or options, it is possible to create an all-inclusive, highly rigorous, and *equitable* environment in schools. If we again consider the football analogy, we can imagine that it is possible for the boys and girls to play in the same game with gender-specific equipment and coaching, coed teams, or a modification of the game to flag football. Of course, if socialization practices are critiqued and challenged in addition, the young women players will not only have the skills and support needed to be successful—they will also have the confidence and societal support important to attain recognition in a game traditionally dominated by men.

Responsive education requires an awareness of differences and an adaptation to meet the needs of diverse learners as they "play the game" of school. In practice, this does not mean dumbing down curriculum, setting lower expectations for performance, or suggesting that students who drop out of school don't have what it takes to succeed. Instead, it means teaching students the skills they need to interpret a rigorous curriculum. It also means holding high standards for our students and ourselves as teachers and community members. It means recognizing that in a just and democratic society, it is not acceptable to cut half of the team.

MYTH #3: MULTICULTURAL EDUCATION IS ONLY FOR NONDOMINANT GROUP STUDENTS

Background of the Myth

The third myth is closely related to the second in that it views multicultural education as something beyond the mainstream. Some people may view multicultural education as a luxury—especially if such courses are offered as electives for students. As long as the school is financially capable, as long as faculty are willing and able to teach multicultural courses or topics, and as long as test scores continue to demonstrate growth at or above that of comparable schools, multicultural education may receive support. Once budget cuts, staffing pressures, or increased academic expectations affect the school, the programs that are viewed as extra or outside of the basic, standard view of schooling are often the first to be eliminated.[5]

Such a perspective suggests that multicultural education is outside of the realm of normal and necessary. It is nice to have around, but expendable and frivolous when the reality of tough times materializes. Similarly, if multicultural education is viewed as supportive for students who are below the testing bar or who need help transitioning to the English-only environment, it does not seem to affect the majority of students. It is easier to justify a cut or change that impacts a small number of students if the action results in benefitting the majority.

This utilitarian perspective is especially problematic when considered within the context of the U.S. public education system. As we know from earlier chapters in this book, the nondominant culture of students who are not White, middle-class, English-speaking, *and* Christian is expanding and will soon surpass the "majority" in terms of numbers. Schools and communities are changing. As a result, educational practices should also change and adapt.

Aside from the changing demographic justification, U.S. educators and stakeholders have an ethical imperative to support multicultural education for all students. As discussed in Chapter 3, multicultural education can provide students and communities with the human relations skills to communicate with increasingly diverse neighbors. Going further, responsive educators recognize that multicultural education lives up to the promise of democracy in education. If, as a nation, we claim to value diverse perspectives and to

encourage all people to become informed of the whole picture and to participate actively in the democracy, our schools should strive to do the same. In
many ways, schools mirror the larger society. Furthermore, schools can *shape*
that larger society. Multicultural education simultaneously prepares learners
to engage in a diverse democracy and encourages them to critique injustices
within the existing society.

It is for this reason that multicultural education is particularly important for
students and communities who do not see themselves as part of the minority.
Research demonstrates that all students benefit from learning how to think
critically within cross-cultural and multimodal contexts.[6] Furthermore, studies
shows that while nondominant culture students are aware of cultural differences and the potential resulting injustices, dominant culture students are less
aware of the continued challenges, possibly due to the culture neutral stance
of parents and educators.[7] Many students (and parents) today believe that the
United States has beaten racism. In reality, racial and religious tensions have
escalated in recent years, making multicultural education extremely important
today.

Another reason that people resist multicultural education stems from the
belief that it increases divisiveness between dominant and nondominant
culture groups. If the view is that multicultural education is secondary to the
main education, then this myth may be true. In that light, nondominant culture
students are separated from dominant culture students for certain courses. It is
somewhat natural to develop an *us* and *them* mindset in such a situation.

If, however, multicultural education is truly comprehensive, then groups of
students are not segregated. The goal in that case is to promote cross-cultural
responsiveness and to encourage civic engagement in communities where
multiple groups come together. Given the reality that many dominant culture
students are unaware of the continued influence of discrimination in today's
society, multicultural education is important as a means to prepare informed
members of our democracy.

Parents, teachers, and other community members may view multicultural
education as a racial (that is, a Black and White) issue. It is important to realize that *all* schools, communities, and classrooms are diverse places—even if
the diversity is not immediately visible. In addition to skin color, students are
different in terms of religious beliefs, linguistic heritage, gender, dis/ability,
economic status, sexual identity, and geographic ties, in addition to countless
other aspects of cultural identity. Sometimes this broad awareness of diversity can seem overwhelming—what doesn't fall beneath the multicultural
education umbrella?

As a result, it is tempting for some teachers to treat diversity as interest-
driven. Such teachers may encourage students to share their hobbies or

holiday traditions, but the same teachers may shy away from topics such as religious practices or mistreatment as related to skin color. As described in Chapter 3, such approaches fit within Banks' first two levels of curriculum integration—they are additive at best. Truly responsive education recognizes that *culture* and *diversity* cannot always (if ever) be chosen. Instead of a focus on individual decision-making and meritocracy, critical multicultural education recognizes that identity is complex and determined by more than the individual. Such identity is not a preference or even an orientation. It is a way of life, and, as such, it cannot be separated from education.

Some stakeholders believe that a student's identity is so personal, complex, and varied that only the family and specific cultural community can respectfully teach about it. Most teachers recognize the importance of honoring the families of their students, so they may worry that if they teach about diverse perspectives they will make a mistake or step on the toes of cultural leaders. Some teachers take this view further: They envision their role in terms of teaching "common" content or mainstream knowledge, while communities and families have the responsibility to teach about culture and diversity.

In some ways, this concern rises from fear of the unknown. As educators, we are more comfortable teaching certain topics than others. If we are cultural outsiders, we may not feel comfortable teaching about diverse knowledge and ways of knowing. In addition, many cultural views overlap with religious beliefs, and we have, as professional educators, been told repeatedly to dance around issues that may blur the line between church and state. We also avoid such topics because if we bring race, religion, and social justice to the attention of our students, we may encourage students to critique education as a whole and our own teaching specifically. We worry that we may be called racist—either by the nondominant culture students/parents who disagree with our teaching of culturally sensitive material or by the dominant culture students/parents who think we are giving preferential treatment to nondominant culture students.

At times, it seems like teachers face a no-win situation when it comes to multicultural education. To avoid the controversy, we ignore differences. These differences are very apparent to students, but without recognition of diversity and questioning of resulting differential treatment, the achievement gap continues to widen, democratic principles grow stagnant, and our potential to innovate as a nation diminishes.

Challenging the Myth

Since multicultural education is important for *all* students, it should be comprehensively integrated across subject areas and grade levels. This task may seem daunting to the financially challenged school district, to veteran teachers with limited experience with diversity and innovative instruction, or to the seemingly heterogeneous community. It is difficult to justify change when facing budget cuts or when you've only experienced dominant culture models of learning yourself. Where do you begin?

The first step in transforming your school district to one that values multicultural education is to connect with the families and communities of diverse students. In forming these connections, it is essential to recognize diversity as an expansive topic. It is also important to learn about groups within your community that are facing discrimination or injustice, since those concepts play a central role in critical and responsive education. Talking to parents, elders, leaders, students, counselors, and social workers can open the door to increased awareness. What "groups" exist in our community and schools? How do the groups view each other? Where are the injustices?

During these conversations, teachers and administrators should strive to learn about appropriate ways for teachers who are cultural outsiders to integrate diverse knowledge and ways of knowing into their teaching. Collaborative planning, curriculum teams that involve community leaders, and culturally focused instructional coaching all offer possibilities in terms of this step in the process.

* * *

While students, teachers, and community members find themselves spending substantial time thinking and talking about the multicultural education myths that are cooked up in today's educational, political, and social spheres, these myths tend to center upon common areas of challenge. Some people worry that multicultural education will add to overburdened systems. Some wonder if multicultural education is simply a political effort to appease nondominant group people, and fear that implementing multicultural education will actually increase the achievement gap if it waters down learning. Some struggle to see the relevance or value for all students given the ever-increasing academic expectations for students and ever-diminishing resources for teachers and schools. As teachers, administrators, parents, and community members, we need straightforward, practical solutions that will improve learning for many students with very little added cost.

When we put these central myths on the table to explore and discuss, we learn several important realities. First, we discover that multicultural education is meant to broaden the existing curriculum—not replace it. Ideally, this will include a comprehensive and critical array of understandings, as suggested by Sleeter and Grant (2009) in their "multicultural social justice education" model. However, it is important to note that frequent, small connections are better than no connections.

Second, we learn that multicultural education, when it is comprehensive and critical, enhances rigor for students. Multicultural education may not be appropriate if *solely* used in remedial or language transition programs. Multicultural should not translate to "watered down" or basic. Along these lines, teachers should carefully critique their own determination of rigor in terms of content, instructional approaches, and assessments. Often, we believe something is rigorous because it is closely tied to tradition and cultural capital—in reality, there are many ways to think about *rigor*.

Third, we recognize that multicultural education is truly for *all* students. When we ask students to consider multiple perspectives, to utilize a variety of approaches to learning, and to demonstrate understanding through diverse forms of assessment, we reinforce higher level thinking, we acknowledge the reality that students are curious about human differences, and we directly confront the misconceptions that challenge democratic principles. We refuse to track our students into "dummy classes" or to cut students from our team.

NOTES

1. See Bourdieu, & Passeron, 1977. Also, see Banks & McGee Banks, 2010, and Nieto & Bode, 2008.
2. Sinner, 2010.
3. See, for example, Danielson, 2007; Marzano, Pickering, & Pollock, 2005; and, Willis, 2006.
4. Gay, 2000; Reyhner, 2002.
5. National Indian Education Association, 2005.
6. American Association of University Women, 1992; Anderson, 1997.
7. See, for example, Harris-Britt, Valrie, & Kurtz-Costes, 2007, and Katz, 2003.

Chapter 7

The Rooftop—Promising Practices and Future Directions

Even if you are committed to responsive education, implementation can seem daunting given the prevalence of obstacles and misconceptions. Despite the challenges, real educators and community members are advancing critical multicultural education every day. This chapter illustrates the theory supporting responsive social justice education by sharing real examples of such education in practice. These promising practices demonstrate ways teachers, students, parents, and scholars are advancing the field of multicultural education, and they provide models and guides for schools and communities who are striving to transform learning for all students.

These examples include community-centered learning, youth participatory action research, critical literacy efforts, and social justice-focused schools. This chapter explores multicultural education for social justice within the context of several of these promising programs, and then provides an overview of general practices that educators can utilize to transform their own schools to centers of engaged learning for action. In this way, we ask you to come with us to the rooftop of multicultural education, to think about the future, the possibilities evident in holding the highest expectations, and to consider the dreams we hold for our students, our teachers, our schools, our communities, and our nation.

VALUING THE COMMUNITY CULTURAL CAPITAL OF STUDENTS

In general, many of the most innovative programs that engage students in multicultural education for social justice focus on the concept of "community cultural capital" and "household funds of knowledge."[1] While cultural capital often refers exclusively to dominant culture knowledge and ways of knowing, and is therefore inherently exclusionary and elitist, community cultural capital recognizes the value of multiple perspectives and community knowledge. In a diverse and democratic nation, community cultural capital encourages many views without privileging one view over another in order to maintain existing power structures. As such, recognition and support of community cultural capital in learning environments goes beyond expanding our collective understanding—it cultivates innovation, advances social justice, and fosters academic, personal, and cultural growth.

Recognizing the value of community cultural capital requires teachers, administrators, and other educational stakeholders to accept several tenets. First, it demands a willingness to learn from community members and students. For some educators, this is very challenging. For generations, teaching has focused primarily on content expertise, not on pedagogical collaboration or a holistic understanding of content.

Second, if they accept the concept of community cultural capital, educational stakeholders must critique the popular concepts of "best practices" and "scientifically based research." As it currently stands, community cultural capital is valued very little in these concepts—at least as they are utilized in the national educational arenas. According to the qualifications for scientifically based research, program results and concepts must be able to transfer from one setting or population to another. In other words, what works in urban Chicago should, theoretically, work in rural Wyoming, if the process is tested carefully. While this example oversimplifies the requirement, it is easy to see why school administrators and trustees often gravitate toward the popular, large curriculum programs.

These are, of course, extreme examples. Research is rarely generalizeable on a nationwide scale, even if it draws upon a large sample and carefully developed experimental design. Unfortunately, many educational stakeholders either do not realize this, or they ignore it. Many schools and districts adopt curriculum, standardize instructional methods, or utilize specific nationally developed tests based simply on published research that claims these approaches are scientifically based or that they reflect best practices in education. Critical stakeholders must carefully examine the research within the context of their specific community. By definition, community cultural capital is not necessarily generalizeable to the broader context of education, but that does not mean such capital should be ignored within a transformative process of school improvement.

Those who support multicultural education that advances social justice often challenge the very ideas that support scientifically based research and best practices work. They argue that such studies often rely heavily upon standardized test scores that are inherently biased toward dominant culture curriculum, instruction, and assessment. In some cases, the programs outlined in this chapter directly resist standardized tests as measures of student success. These programs focus on comprehensive measures of success; they boast increased student retention and graduation, increased college attendance, increased cultural sustainability, increased economic opportunities, and—often—increased test scores.

This holistic view of success is tied to the final requirement for educational stakeholders who value community cultural capital: We must shift our mindsets regarding success and failure. Traditionally, U.S. educators, parents, school board members, administrators, and policy makers have focused on student failure, whether that failure is linked to test scores or drop-out statistics. Believing in community cultural capital demands attention to what students and community members bring with them to the learning environment—not on what they are missing or lacking. With this new view, teachers can build upon student strengths, and they can utilize strengths to address areas of weakness, as opposed to drill and kill methods that focus exclusively on addressing weaknesses in isolation.

The "drill and kill" teaching approach, which focuses on relentless repetition of basic skills for the purpose of boosting test scores, leads to student frustration, discourages critical thinking, and is inconsistent with an education for social justice. In recent years, we've seen an increased focus on low-level skills that target the weaknesses identified by standardized tests. Nondominant culture students are overrepresented in classes and programs that focus on such approaches. While some short-term gains may be made, studies suggest long-term growth is compromised, student interest decreases, creativity diminishes, and cultural connectivity declines under these programs.

Two Examples

To bring the ideas of community cultural capital to life, we wish to illuminate the work of Tara Yosso (2006) as described in her book *Critical Race Counterstories Along the Chicana/o Pipeline*. Yosso wanted to address a critique directed at parents of Latina/o school children, which claimed the parents did not value education. Educators used as evidence of this lack of support that parents did not have many books in their home, that they did not help their children with their homework, and that most did not attend parent-teacher conferences or other school-wide events. Of course, a myriad of reasons can explain some of these actions.[2]

Rather than focusing on what parents were NOT doing to support their children's education, Yosso decided to ask parents how they saw themselves supporting that education. Often via *consejos*, or advice giving via stories, parables, or direct messages, these parents mentioned six ways they help their children academically, though these are often unnoticed by most educators.

The parents communicated *aspirational capital*, described as holding high their dreams and hopes for their children's futures even when obvious barriers might stand in their way. *Linguistic capital* included the skills and knowledge children learned through their home language and an appreciation of the value of being bilingual. The parents helped their children via *navigational capital*, information shared with their children about how to maneuver through social institutions. *Social capital* was the ways these parents taught their children to rely on the network of friends, family, and community resources to move ahead. Parents used their *familial capital* to help their children have a sense of history, a sense of belonging, and a sense of cultural intuition about their world. Finally, Yosso described parents' use of *resistance capital*, understood as the skills and abilities to challenge social inequalities that their children are likely to face. It would be difficult to imagine any child not benefiting from bringing these forms of community cultural capital into the classroom.

It is also important to recognize the *cultural* in community cultural capital. That is, this communal capital that parents bring and children learn is rooted in the cultural community to which they belong. Maria Fránquiz and Maria del Carmen Salazar (2004) provide a clear picture of how students in a high school employ distinctly Mexican cultural value orientations to help them navigate through their education experiences. In addition to using *consejos* (sharing of advice with each other), students also drew upon *confianza*, a trust and faith in themselves and their peers. These students also demonstrated *respeto*, respect for themselves and for others in the school setting. Finally, Fránquiz and Salazar described how the students incorporated *coraje*, courage and passion, to help sustain them through their educational experiences.

The programs we outline in this chapter turn the social justice tables in several ways. First, they engage students as co-developers of knowledge, content, and curriculum. Second, they center the local community within the learning process. Third, they value nondominant culture knowledge and ways of knowing, including the various funds of knowledge and types of cultural capital diverse learners draw upon in their daily and academic lives. Finally, they engage teachers as life-long learners and team players.

PROMISING DIRECTIONS IN MULTICULTURAL, SOCIAL JUSTICE EDUCATION

Community-Centered Learning: Youth PAR using Doc Your Bloc(k) and PhotoVoice

One of the core tenets of critical multicultural education for social justice is a recentering of the community in the educational process. Historically, humans have often learned in community contexts. In terms of social justice work, community-based activism has frequently spurred regional and national level reform. Despite the role that communities have played, and continue to play, in the lives of students, they are being left out of the process of curriculum design, educational planning, and student assessment more and more frequently. Increased emphasis on national standards, high-stakes testing, and federal-level policies have shifted the focus of education away from the community.

Critical multicultural education recognizes the importance of community in student learning in several ways. First, differences cannot, and should not, be ignored. Community norms, expectations, and histories all shape the experiences students have when they enter school, and they continue to shape learning for those students during and after their schooling. Second, ignoring the knowledge systems and ways of knowing of communities privileges dominant culture ideology. As addressed in Chapter 6, such a perspective not only limits the innovative potential of the United States as a whole, but it also conflicts with the principles of democracy.

Community-centered learning repositions the community within the educational process. Community members identify important knowledge, areas of need, and appropriate levels of teacher involvement. Students engage in learning that connects to community issues, occurs in the authentic environment of the community, and contributes to the improvement of the community—in community terms instead of the dominant culture terms—as a whole.

Many successful multicultural education programs draw upon community-centered learning to some extent. In some cases, community leaders serve on curriculum selection teams. In others, teachers partner with community members to provide instruction. In still others, classes occur in community-based settings as a means to promote "place conscious education."[3]

Some of the most powerful community-centered models utilize "Youth Participatory Action Research" (Youth PAR).[4] Youth PAR engages students in the identification and investigation of a community challenge. Students learn the principles of action research within community specific contexts and through culturally responsive frameworks. They practice those principles in authentic settings, conducting interviews with community members and documenting their learning through audio, visual, and/or written media. Following the data gathering, the students interpret and analyze the data, organize their findings, and share their results in authentic settings.

Examples of critical Youth PAR include the Doc Your Block projects initiated in schools and communities in Oakland and Chicago.[5] Teachers guide students through the process of selecting a research question, learning about critical inquiry and theory, and applying new skills to the challenges students see in their own neighborhoods. The students gather data and document the challenges in their communities using digital videocameras. Upon their return to the classroom, students carefully and critically interpret the data, edit film clips, explore possible solutions, and prepare a presentation for community members. The products are often shared locally and nationally in both formal and informal contexts. For example, Doc Your Block projects may be posted to YouTube where they can be viewed by thousands of people, and they may also be shared with smaller audiences at professional conferences or in the local neighborhoods. The students' work has resulted in publications, new initiatives, and solutions.

Similar projects utilize digital still cameras and/or voice recorders to construct "Photo Voice" projects.[6] While students are often encouraged to investigate an area that interests them specifically, teachers and adult community members sometimes provide a topic area to explore. For example, in one Native community people were interested in determining access to healthy foods, so students and elders used PhotoVoice to investigate the availability of fresh produce and locally raised meat in reservation grocery stores. The projects documented limited access to high-quality foods, spurring students to think about the connections between transportation costs (to reach a medium-sized grocery store, reservation residents must travel to border town communities) and health (the reservation residents face higher rates of diabetes and heart disease than people who live off the reservation). As a result, several schools have started school gardens and elders have started working with teachers to share knowledge of traditional foods.

In both Doc Your Block and PhotoVoice, the focus rests on engaging students and community members in the telling of their stories. Historically, many of these stories have been silenced by dominant culture views of curriculum, but these stories are extremely powerful when considering the influence of social justice on communities and students. In addition, Youth PAR introduces students to academic skills and concepts, including qualitative research analysis, critical theory, and formal inquiry. Students are asked to truly *see* their neighborhoods and communities in multiple ways in order to advance social justice.

The critical emphasis of Youth PAR is particularly important, and it distinguishes the approach from other forms of problem-based learning. Some teachers guide students through a highly structured research process that analyzes community problems through the lens of dominant culture knowledge exclusively. Youth PAR facilitators engage students in critical inquiry, which requires students to deconstruct understanding of challenges in various ways. Metacognition plays a significant role in the process, and students are encouraged to question their teacher, adults, and others in and beyond the community.

Within this process, students are not necessarily encouraged to privilege one perspective over others. In addition to learning academic skills, students are also expected to develop civic and cultural skills. They learn how to appropriately interact with members of the community based upon cultural norms, they participate in the process of developing and proposing solutions, and they learn about ways to become holistically informed members of society. As a result, they gain skills needed to participate in democracy on multiple levels.

Teachers, administrators, and other educational stakeholders can learn from Youth PAR in many ways. First, it is important for educational stakeholders to engage in their own Participatory Action Research. When developing new curricula, expanding instructional methods, and selecting assessment tools, stakeholders should conduct community-centered participatory research to determine community needs and interests, as well as the existing practices and beliefs of other teachers, administrators, and school board members. In addition, teachers and administrators who are cultural outsiders can learn extensively from Youth PAR projects, since students—as cultural insiders—often have unique access to topics and experiences. Finally, students and teachers can co-construct new understanding about challenges both in and beyond the community through in-depth critical analysis or critical service learning.

Critical Literacy: Spoken Word, Indigenous Storywork, and Digital Testimonio

Like Youth Participatory Action Research and other forms of community-centered learning, critical literacy projects focus on hearing the story-experiences of students and community members who are not members of the dominant culture. Historically, these stories have been excluded from textbooks, classroom conversations, and standardized tests.

Furthermore, privileged story-experiences have, historically, been most frequently shared through reading and writing. These two forms of literacy have served the purpose of preserving and spreading dominant culture information. Other forms of literacy, such as oral, visual, and kinesthetic forms of communication, may be more responsive in terms of sharing nondominant culture experiences. For example, many Indigenous peoples traditionally shared knowledge through oral storytelling, dance, or weaving.

These forms of communication—these forms of literacy—are often excluded from schools, or they are shared only as electives or as part of the "Foods and Festivals" approaches to multicultural education. Educational stakeholders who utilize critical literacy practices chip away at the perspective that dominant culture knowledge and ways of knowing should overshadow community understanding and cultural approaches to learning. Furthermore, these educational stakeholders realize that alternative literacy practices can strengthen conventional literacy, increase critical thinking across content areas, and engage students who historically have resisted standard literacy education.

Critical literacy, as a field, arises from the recognition that story-experiences can—and must—be shared by diverse peoples in various ways in order to advance social justice. In a literature course, this means that students should review texts (both written and unwritten) created by members of various nondominant cultures. Most importantly, this study and exploration should engage students in asking questions about power as connected to culture, socioeconomic class, and levels of "literacy" as defined through traditional means. For example, students may explore the sociocultural meaning of graffiti, consider the messages communicated by the body language of a nondominant culture actor in a film, or discuss the accuracy of a Nigerian woman's story as told by a White British anthropologist.

Critical literacy is heavily influenced by various forms of critical theory, including critical race theory (CRT).[7] CRT emerged in the 1970s as a means to consider the meaning and importance of property and capital in legal studies. Within the field of education, CRT theorists consider the role of intellectual property and cultural capital in learning, power, and change. CRT proponents argue that dominant culture knowledge and ways of knowing are often privileged in textbooks, classrooms, and tests.

Therefore, certain students who have automatic access to the "capital" or property, as a result of membership in the dominant culture, have increased opportunity. One way to confront such bias, which the theorists argue is endemic within society, is to include—and potentially to privilege—the "counter-story"[8] of the "Cultural Other."[9] Critical literacy generally, and CRT specifically, materializes in educational practice in many ways. Teachers can engage students in sharing counterstories or in utilizing alternative forms of literacy such as digital technology or spoken word poetry.

One example of alternative literacy that advances critical theory is the use of digital storytelling. For example, several Latinas at the University of Utah have generated digital *testimonios* to share their counter-stories and work to advance social justice in the Salt Lake City community.[10] These stories combine potent experiences with visual images and music. In addition to sharing the counterstory, representations such as digital story reach expansive audiences—not just academic audiences.

Another way educators and scholars can engage students, teachers, and community members in critical literacy practices is through the inclusion of spoken word, hip-hop performance, and poetry slams. In these events, performers share their own work, or the work of critical artists, in authentic settings. These forums serve not only as spaces for the sharing of counter-stories, but also for the critical examination of the intersections of art, music, and story as a means to shape understanding.

Indigenous scholars often encourage teachers to integrate stories of elders and other tribal members into their teaching. One example of this is through "indigenous storywork," which connects traditional story and knowledge with skills and concepts in the school setting.[11] Furthermore, indigenous storywork builds upon important cultural values, including respect, reverence, and interrelatedness. Such storywork requires connections between content areas, topics, and members of the community.

In general, critical literacy practices encourage students and teachers to think about *story* and *experience* in different ways. Instead of privileging written accounts shared by members of the dominant culture, critical literacy demands attention to counterstory and alternative representations of story-experience. Such practices emphasize that literacy and communication are holistic and dynamic experiences that require understanding of cultural norms, recognition of differences in perspectives, awareness of audience and purpose, and critical self-evaluation in terms of bias and preconceived expectations. In addition, critical literacy allows teachers to connect to students and communities in meaningful ways. Finally, critical literacy challenges the larger societal views of literacy, knowledge, and representation in a way that encourages critical thinking, creative expression, and the advancement of social justice.

Teachers and other educational stakeholders can advocate for critical literacy practices in their own schools in several ways. First, it is important to determine the type of stories that are included in the existing curriculum, and the nature of the stories that are excluded. In some cases, curriculum resources dictate the nature of the content, while in others, teachers choose the material. Responsive educators can work with students and community members to identify or record counterstories. It is important to note that in some cultures, certain experiences cannot be told or distributed by cultural outsiders or during certain times of the year.

In addition, teachers, administrators, and community members should consider the way counterstories are shared. Since written print is often equated with colonizing or oppressive discourse, elitist education, and legal speak, schools should strive to develop a balanced approach that incorporates reading, writing, speaking, listening, digital media, kinesthetic communication, art, music, etc. It is also important to consider the structure of traditional literacy activities themselves. Often, as literacy educators, we ask students to brainstorm for a writing project using writing (such as making an outline or creating a concept map).

Responsive teachers engage learners in the process of writing through various learning modalities and communication forms. For example, students may brainstorm using an art project, they may revise by reading their paper out loud to a peer, and they may present their paper using multimedia technology. Utilizing various approaches builds on student strengths, challenges the narrow definition of literacy, and, according to brain-based educational research, reinforces ideas and concepts for all learners.

FREIRIAN VIEWS OF LEARNING: SCHOOL-COMMUNITY PARTNERSHIPS AND SOCIAL JUSTICE SCHOOLS

Most, if not all, of the projects described in this chapter have been influenced by the work of Brazilian educator Paulo Freire (1972/2000). Freire argued that both the oppressor and the oppressed can influence the nature of power in education. Through education, Freire explained, the oppressed can gain access to and transform the influence of the dominant culture. The critical consciousness—or *conscientization*—that results from educational self-empowerment advances social justice.

Freire also emphasized that educational pedagogy and political ideology are closely linked. Basic facts and dominant culture knowledge contribute to, Freire would argue, the *banking model* of education where knowledge and ideologies are "deposited," which reinforces class divisions and fails to prepare oppressed students for anything other than a basic industrial or service job. Responsive, critical educators—and their students—must confront and deconstruct the banking model in their own communities and institutions.

Today, Freire's work continues, even in seemingly advanced countries like the United States. As discussed in previous chapters, significant gaps exist between cultural and socioeconomic groups in this country. Despite the belief that is widespread among middle-class Euro-Americans that Americans are becoming increasingly accepting of diversity, the gaps continue to widen in schools. In order to advance social justice, schools and communities must cooperate on multiple levels, and students and community members must have a voice in the design, implementation, and evaluation of educational processes. The oppressed must become conscious of the oppression in order to critique it, deconstruct it, challenge it, and change it.

Several projects have demonstrated the potential for Freirian practices to ignite learning for students and to advance change in communities. On a basic level, school-community partnerships offer a model for starting to transform pedagogy. In these collaborative settings, schools can partner with community members to explore curriculum, coach teachers in instructional practices, and design holistic assessment tools. Some schools have hired cultural mentors or instructional coaches who work closely with teachers to integrate cultural knowledge and ways of knowing into curriculum and instruction. Other schools utilize grandparent programs or similar approaches, which involve community members as teaching assistants in the classroom. Many schools offer community education services, such as family literacy programs, to the larger community. At the university level, several institutions have dedicated social justice support systems for scholars and teachers.[12]

Finally, several small schools have adopted a Freirian-type mission as part of their holistic view of learning. Some of these schools focus on integrating culture and learning, while others emphasize social justice in general. For example, the Native American Community Academy (NACA) in Albuquerque, New Mexico, is a public charter school that connects to culture through in-depth, interdisciplinary learning. NACA centers learning upon extensive language coursework (Navajo, Lakota, and Spanish) and experiential, community-based learning. Cutting-edge technology, an extensive arts program, and rigorous college preparation further bolster NACA's reputation as a leader within critical multicultural education practice.

NACA's success is not isolated. Other small schools and specialized, community-focused learning programs have experienced similar results in terms of implementing critical multicultural education. These programs all utilize high expectations, employ dedicated and qualified teachers who are eager to learn from and collaborate with community members and students, and connect students to culture, language, and community in meaningful ways. From the Harlem Success Academy to the Greater Lawndale Little Village School for Social Justice in Chicago to dual-immersion bilingual education programs in a variety of states to the Council of Youth Research in LA, many models exist to guide the work we do in our own schools and communities.

* * *

These programs provide inspiration on many levels. If complete reform and curricular overhaul seem unrealistic, these projects offer ideas for incremental changes as well. The central concepts of community-centered learning, critical literacy practices, and social justice education are transferrable to many contexts. See Table 7.1 for a few ideas to help guide change at various levels in your own schools and communities.

In general, educational stakeholders who are interested in implementing multicultural education and advancing opportunities for all students focus on

Table 7.1   Practices for transformation.

Quality	Initial	Developing	Critical
Caring Relationships	• Maintain small class sizes & small schools • Utilize journaling & conferencing • Participate in home visits	• Partner teachers with cultural mentors • Involve teachers in community-based learning • Utilize peer mentoring programs • Use "looping"	• Engage community members in planning & evaluation • Provide authentic formats for students & teachers to collaborate
Rigorous Connections	• Integrate standards with multicultural curriculum • Keep a teaching journal to monitor teaching successes & areas of challenge	• Develop high-level, culturally responsive curriculum • Collaborate with experts in the field to evaluate programs • Connect community & academic "capital" during field experiences	• Engage students in community-centered action research • Connect students to post-secondary opportunities through digital learning, site visits, & community member mentors
Meaningful Experiences	• Connect to student interests • Attend & participate in extracurricular & community events • Add cultural curriculum to all content areas	• Connect curriculum to culture & community in comprehensive ways • Engage in community-based professional development	• Engage students in community-centered learning • Work with community members to determine & implement meaningful connections

developing caring relationships with students, promoting engaging learning experiences that are connected to students' cultural identities and community, and cultivating high expectations for student learning. Such individuals believe in their students, in themselves, and in the communities, and they build upon strengths in order to confront challenges and advance social justice. Our dream for students, schools, and educational stakeholders relies upon these understandings.

As we lie on the rooftop of the home we call multicultural education, we look at the stars and the rising moon. We think about the tomorrows ahead for us. We hope that in these tomorrows, each and every child will feel valued for his/her unique identity, encouraged to use his/her strengths, able to learn about his/her cultural community through culturally responsive instruction, and allowed to share his/her understanding through holistic and meaningful approaches.

NOTES

1. Moll, 1992.
2. See Rios, 2009.
3. See Gruenewald, 2003, and Powers, 2004.
4. See Cammarota & Fine, 2008, and DuncanAndrade, 2008.
5. See DuncanAndrade, 2008, and Stovall, Calderon, Carrera, & King, 2009.
6. Minkler & Wallerstein, 2003.
7. See Ladson-Billings & Tate, 1995; Vaught & Castagno, 2008; and, Zamudio, Russell, Rios & Bridgeman, 2011.
8. See Ladson-Billings & Tate, 1995, and Vaught & Castagno, 2008.
9. Montecinos, 1995.
10. Flores & Garcia, 2009.
11. Archibald, 2008.
12. See the University of Washington Center for Multicultural Education (http://education.washington.edu/cme/) and the University of Wyoming Social Justice Research Center (http://www.uwyo.edu/sjrc/).

Chapter 8

The Tool Shed

Resources to Extend Your Knowledge

Recall the way you learned to ride a bike, play tennis, or drive a car. For the vast majority of us, we did not one day just get on a bike and start riding. We did not look at the first tennis racket we ever saw and begin hitting overhand serves. And we would be scared at the prospect of a person driving a car the very first time that they entered one.

Rather, much of the way we learned to ride a bike, play a game, or drive a car occurs via careful observation of models provided by people who are experts at the task to be learned. We are then supported in our initial efforts to engage in the task at hand: training wheels and then a caregiver running along side of us, gradually letting go as we learned to ride a bike. Finally, we incorporate these abilities into our knowledge systems ("gradually press on the gas as you slowly let out the clutch," we think to ourselves), as these abilities become part of our core identities ("I'm a bike rider, tennis player, and car driver").

The field of education had been dominated by theories of learning largely based in the field of psychology. The vast majority of these theories focused on the individual and what occurs inside someone's head as he/she is learning. However, as the opening examples of this chapter suggest, there is a much greater social dimension to our learning than we often recognize and appreciate. Most recently, educational theorists, guided most centrally by the work of Lev Vygotsky (1978), have come to understand the social dimension of how we come to know.

For those educators, then, who are interested in pursuing a social justice-oriented multicultural education and making it a part of who they are, it is comforting to know that there are examples of people working to implement multicultural education in meaningful ways. There are also tools, like training wheels in our example, and support systems that will enable their first efforts. Finally, as they are achieving productive results, there are professional communities to which teachers can belong, in order to learn more and to solidify their identities about who they are as multicultural, social justice educators.

Likewise, using the metaphor of a house that we have used throughout, we have been suggesting that multicultural education has a solid foundation of walls, rooms, and rooftops from which to consider hopes and dreams. But this house is not yet completed. In some instances, new additions need to be constructed as new subfields of interest within multicultural education come into view. Sometimes, it might be a matter of adding new details to what already exists in order to provide a more complete picture of a topic or issue being addressed within the field. And even once in a while, as we learn to see things with a new lens, we need to repair what we originally had constructed.

Multicultural education is a dynamic (changing) field of study. It is dynamic since new scholarly work is being produced consistently. It is dynamic because education professionals are enacting its principles in new ways everyday. And it is dynamic because our society is constantly changing as new issues, challenges, and opportunities arise within the nation-state.

In this final chapter, we provide you, the readers, with some tools to help extend your knowledge and thinking about multicultural education. These are tools to help you construct, add, or repair existing understandings around diversity in education. The intent here is not to provide an exhaustive list of resources, but to include what we consider some of the best, most essential books, journals, Web sites, and professional organizations that you might consider if you are interested in knowing more and staying informed about the field of multicultural education.

Before beginning, we want to reiterate that these are the tools that we most wish to recommend to you but that someone else might not think are quite so important. For them, some other tools would be more highly recommended for your tool shed. Recall that one principle of multicultural education is the inherent value of diverse viewpoints.

We also will highlight those resources that are focused on multicultural or social justice education generally. In doing so, we do not provide description of the many resources dedicated to specific social groups (based on race, ethnicity, sexual orientation, gender, or dis/ability condition). Also, it does not describe content specific resources (for example, multicultural math or children's literature). Notwithstanding, we recommend these tools as a beginning place.

Fortunately, we are assisted in considering which tools to recommend by multicultural education scholar Paul Gorksi. In 2010, Gorski conducted a survey asking over 200+ multicultural education specialists about their recommendations on a variety of things from books, to Web sites, to professional organizations. We felt these recommendations were informative and recommend a visit to the Web site where you can find the complete lists for yourself.[1] While we don't provide the complete list below, what we do provide is a list of what we consider the most essential resources and a short description of what you will find there.

INTRODUCTORY BOOKS

As we suggested earlier in this book, James Banks is often described as one founder of multicultural education as a contemporary academic discipline. Therefore, his book *Multicultural Education: Issues and Perspectives*, with Cherry McGee Banks (2010), is on our list of essential readings. In this edited volume, Banks and McGee Banks bring together some of the leading experts in the field to write chapters about the meaning of diversity and the ways in which multicultural education is understood broadly. It focuses on a variety of different forms of diversity including religious, social class, gender, exceptionality, and linguistic. In addition, chapters highlight school and classroom level practices including curriculum and instruction considerations.

Christine Sleeter and Carl Grant's (2009) book, *Making Choices for Multicultural Education: Five Approaches to Race, Class and Gender*, is another must read for those interested in knowing more about the field. After an introduction that describes "business as usual," the authors detail five different ways multicultural education is understood and enacted (we described these approaches in Chapter 3 of this book). At the end of this book, Sleeter and Grant describe their choice and the rationale behind multicultural social justice education. This book is a reminder of the idea that there are many ways to engage in multicultural education.

The third book we recommend, *Affirming Diversity: The Sociopolitical Context of Multicultural Education*, is authored by Sonia Nieto and Patty Bode (2008). This book brings a broader lens to multicultural education as it works to understand multicultural education within the current social and political climate, partly due to its definition of multicultural education, which is one of the most often cited definitions, given its comprehensive focus. This work has an especially strong social justice focus orientation throughout, including specific recommendations for educators interested in pursuing educational and social change. One highlight of this book is the case studies of young people that are sprinkled throughout the text.

The first three books described are textbooks in the traditional sense. These next two works represent two other genres within the field. The first is a study of successful teachers of African American students and is authored by Gloria Ladson-Billings (1994). The book, *The Dreamkeepers: Successful Teachers of African American Children*, profiles these teachers, both White and African American, and provides a description of the way in which these teachers value their students and work to enact teaching approaches that are culturally relevant. It is a mix of both scholarly research and engaging narrative style that makes this a good read.

The final book to be profiled is also written in an engaging narrative style. It is Jonathan Kozol's (1991) *Savage Inequalities*. This book is both an easy read given its storytelling style and a difficult read given the way Kozol brings us into the life of highly segregated and poorly funded schools as contrasted with schools for the wealthy. He provides a detailed account of the conditions in which we expect some of children to learn and asks how these disparities can occur in a county who holds equality as a national ideal. Along with this work, we also recommend any of the other of Kozol's work, but especially *The Shame of a Nation: The Restoration of Apartheid Schooling in America* (2006).

We highlight two books that are especially helpful for the educator who wishes to know how to enact a multicultural, social justice-oriented education in his/her school and classroom. *Beyond Heroes and Holidays: A Practical Guide to K–12 Anti-racist, Multicultural Education and Staff Development* is an edited book by Lee, Menkart, and Okazawa-Rey (1998). Along with engaging articles, it provides examples of lessons that come from teachers who are engaging in multicultural education, including those with an especially strong anti-racist stance.

Additionally, the Rethinking Schools organization has put together two volumes titled *Rethinking Our Classrooms: Teaching for Equity and Justice*.[2] What makes these volumes meaningful are the mix of provocative essays, poetry and photos, classroom based activities, and teacher anecdotes with an explicitly social justice orientation.

EXPERT BOOKS

For those educators and community leaders who are ready for more advanced readings in the field of multicultural education, we offer the following additional resources. The *Handbook of Research on Multicultural Education* by James A. Banks and Cherry McGee Banks (2004) is an edited volume that brings the most notable scholars in the field together to provide the most comprehensive reviews of research available in the field. It provides both broad reviews of research about the field itself, about teaching/learning and education, and about different social groups, and it overviews international efforts being made the field. It is one of the best sources for beginning a scholarly review of some topic related to multicultural education.

The book *Teaching for Diversity and Social Justice* by Maurianne Adams, Lee Anne Bell, and Pat Griffin (2007), along with the companion edited book titled *Readings for Diversity and Social Justice: An Anthology on Racism, Antisemitism, Sexism, Heterosexism, Ableism, and Classism* by Maurianne Adams, Warren J. Blumenfeld, Carmelita Castañeda, Heather Hackman, Madeline Peters, and Ximena Zúñiga (2010) provides some of the best theoretical, conceptual, and practical works for enacting education with a social justice perspective. Targeting higher education and professional development for school-based professionals, these two works provide direction for individuals who are interested in engaging in the difficult work of pursuing a social justice-oriented approach to education.

Almost all who take a critical, social justice-oriented approach to their work around diversity in education would acknowledge the seminal works of Brazilian educator Paulo Freire. Freire's (1972/2000) classic work in the field is titled *Pedagogy of the Oppressed.* In that work, he forged a vision of education that is rooted in the everyday world of workers and in the potential for the oppressed to pose problems and seek solutions, using education as a means to enact those solutions. The pedagogical vision he describes includes the importance of helping students develop a critical consciousness and then employing the skills of social activism to make much needed changes. Another work to consider by Freire includes *Teachers as Cultural Workers: Letters to Those Who Dare to Teach* (1998).

A Different Mirror: A History of Multicultural America by Ronald Takaki (1993) provides an engaging historical account of the diversity in the United States from before the nation's birth to modern times. It is a reminder that multiculturalism has been a hallmark of the United States from its early inception. While focusing on the ways groups have been oppressed, Takaki also details accounts of how groups have worked for their liberation, often forging alliances in doing so.

A related historical account, specific to the history of different social groups' experiences in schools, is Joel Spring's (2009) book *Deculturalization and the Struggle for Equality: A Brief History of the Education of Dominated Cultures in the United States.* That same theme of both oppression and the struggle for freedom is equally evident in this short book.

The final book in our tool shed that we recommend is *Rethinking Multicultural Education: Teaching for Racial and Cultural Justice* edited by Wayne Au (2009). A publication of Rethinking Schools, like the other publications we have highlighted from this organization, this work is provocative and practical. One of the things we most appreciate about the works from Rethinking Schools, evident in this text edited by Au, is the complexity, difficulty, and challenge of doing critical multicultural education. Rather than neat and tidy vignettes of teaching, it shows all the complexity and messiness associated with teaching against the grain.

JOURNALS

An important indication of the strength of any academic field of study is the quality of professional journals dedicated to that area of specialization. We now describe six journals that we feel are representative of the field and that provide current perspectives about issues that emerge within the field.

Equity & Excellence in Education is a journal published at the University of Massachusetts Amherst. It is an academic-focused journal with research studies, both quantitative and qualitative, making up the bulk of articles it publishes. It has a strong social justice focus that includes how understanding both institutional and interpersonal relations play themselves out in both preK–12 schools as well as college and university settings.

Multicultural Perspectives is the journal of the National Association for Multicultural Education (an organization we will profile under organizations). Its primary focus is on multicultural education, especially as it occurs in teacher education programs. While it includes research-based works and position papers aimed at "advancing the conversation," it also includes the practice of multicultural education "in the classroom." It includes alternative formats of knowledge dissemination including narratives, personal perspectives, and reviews of books and films.

Two other journals are much like *Multicultural Perspectives* in that they publish both research and position papers as well as reviews, practical accounts, and personal perspectives. *Multicultural Education* publishes work aimed at the more general education audience. A new addition to the journals in the field is the internet-based *International Journal of Multicultural Education* (formerly the *Electronic Magazine of Multicultural Education*; available at: http://ijme-journal.org/index.php/ijme). Both of these journals have an explicit focus on the field of multicultural education.

Rethinking Schools is a more teacher-directed, teacher-focused journal that has an especially strong focus on critical multicultural education. Originally published in a newspaper format, this journal focuses on the political dimensions of reforming school for diversity and equity in education. The articles it publishes are highly accessible and include teacher-based accounts of teaching for social justice and social change. It has also bundled some of the articles that have appeared in the journal in edited books (two of which were *Rethinking Our Classrooms* and *Rethinking Multicultural Education*, as described above). The Rethinking Schools Web page (http://www.rethinkingschools.org) lists many of the organization's publications, including recent and past issues of their journal.

Teaching Tolerance is a free publication for educators from the Southern Poverty Law Center. It is the most preK–12 teacher-oriented of the journals we have described. It addresses school and classroom level challenges with an especially strong focus on addressing the interpersonal nature of racism and discrimination. Most of the works published are personal accounts of students, teachers, schools, and communities as they struggle to combat bias.

PROFESSIONAL ORGANIZATIONS

One of the trademarks of an academic field of study is the number of professional organizations that it inspires. This is also the case in multicultural education. Professional organizations usually sponsor a conference that brings its members together to become informed, develop networks, share resources, and gain inspiration. We provide here a list of some of the primary organizations with a multicultural education, diversity, and equity agenda.

The National Association for Multicultural Education (NAME) (http://nameorg.org/) is the lead organization surrounding multicultural education. Founded in 1981, NAME has several very strong state chapters as well as a national presence. Its annual conference occurs every fall. NAME is the sponsor of the journal *Multicultural Perspectives*. About 30% of the membership consists of preK–12 teachers; in addition, a small but powerful number of community-based activists are also members as well as some of the most prominent scholars in the field.

The Southern Poverty Law Center (http://www.splcenter.org) is a civil rights-oriented organization that has as its primary focus the elimination of bias and racism as well as the protection of vulnerable and historically marginalized social groups within the United States. As part of its mission, it tracks hate groups and domestic terrorist groups within the United States. It also uses the courts to seek redress when some social injustice has occurred. Finally, it has a strong education arm that helps create the materials and journal *Teaching Tolerance*.

Teaching for Change (http://www.teachingforchange.org/) is an organization committed to bringing about social change via social justice-oriented education with a focus on what can be done in classrooms. It has a strong list of teacher-friendly resources, most for purchase, which can be utilized in schools. Teaching for Change also has a focus on early childhood education as well as parent-based initiatives.

The Matrix Center (http://www.uccs.edu/~matrix/) at the University of Colorado—Colorado Springs, is an organization dedicated to understanding the multiple forms of oppression and their intersections. They host an annual spring conference, the Knapsack Institute, a three-day event directed at understanding social inequality and supporting social justice, especially within teaching and learning.

At this point, we wish to highlight two additional conferences that may be of interest. The White Privilege Conference (http://www.uccs.edu/~wpc/) is held every spring. The focus of the conference is to help attendees understand the nature of White privilege, learn to respect differences, and begin to connect across those lines of difference. It is open to students, parents, teachers, community activists, and other professionals in a variety of fields of work and study.

The National Conference on Race and Ethnicity (http://www.ncore. ou.edu/) is held every year in late spring. It is the largest and oldest conference with a specific focus on race and ethnicity. Its primary focus is higher education and usually draws some of the nation's most provocative community activists and scholars working in the field.

WEB SITES FOR RESOURCES

The number of electronic resources, especially Web sites, has grown substantially in the past decade. These resources provide a variety of support for educators interested in extending their knowledge and understanding of multicultural education. We highlight those Web sites that not only provide access to their published materials, but that provide teaching resources as well.

EdChange/Multicultural Pavilion (http://www.edchange.org) begins our list of these Web sites. *EdChange* is an outlet for educational research, professional development initiatives, and educational resources dedicated to diversity and equity in schools. Besides providing a list of training services available, the Web site provides free access to helpful educational resources that can be used in schools, colleges and universities. It provides a list of publications and related research for those interested in learning more about diversity and equity in schooling.

Teaching Tolerance (http://www.tolerance.org) is a Web site that has its magazine as its anchor. The Web site includes a variety of other materials as well including teaching kits with videos, activities, and reading materials to be used in schools. Recently, the organization has created materials to engage students in activities to "mix it up" by sitting and interacting with other students who are different from themselves. The Web site includes helpful resources for teachers' professional learning and development. Most of the resources are free to educators.

The National Association for Multicultural Education (http://nameorg.org/) Web site primarily lists information related to the organization, from conference information to news from state chapters. But, in addition, the site hosts a very helpful and comprehensive list of resources of interest to educators. These tools include a variety of resources about equity and diversity such as famous speeches, grant information, journals, parent resources, poetry and published sorties, surveys and questionnaires, and research among many other helpful resources.

The National Center for Culturally Responsive Education Systems (http:// www.nccrest.org) is a federally funded center with a focus on diversity and special education. It has a dual focus on closing the achievement gap between White students and nondominant culture students as well as working to eliminate the inappropriate and disproportionate referral of nondominant culture students to special education services. It has recently linked itself with the *Equity Alliance at Arizona State University* (http://www.equityallianceatasu.org), itself a helpful organization with a Web site with important resources and information.

The Web site at the *Freire Project* (http://www.freireproject.org) offers a range of resources for those educational professionals and community activists who are interested in learning more about and seeing the extensions rooted in the works of Paulo Freire. It includes information about conferences, journals, resources (books and videos), and activities helpful to those who wish to pursue a critical multicultural education perspective.

* * *

We hope that this chapter provides a sampling of the many and varied resources—tools for learning, teaching, and leading—that are available to you to advance your efforts to make schools more multicultural in ways that promote both equity and social justice. The work to accomplish this is difficult. But just as with any construction on a house, the tools are just part of the task. It helps to bring in others to support, assist, and offer guidance given their own experiences. We know that finding a home in multicultural education is difficult, but it is helpful to know that you will be joining educators and activists from all over the United States who stand alongside those who are trying to promote education and equity in ways that affirm diversity.

The abolitionist Theodore Parker, in the 1850s spoke these words, as true then as it is today: "The Arc of a moral universe is long, but it bends towards justice."

NOTES

1. Survey results as well as methodology available at: http://www.edchange.org/ survey.html.
2. Au, Bigelow, & Karp, 2007; Bigelow, 2004.

References

Adams, M., Bell, L. A., & Griffin, P. (Eds.) (2007). *Teaching for diversity and social justice*, (2nd ed.). New York: Routledge.

Adams, M., Blumenfeld, W. J., Castañeda, C., Hackman, H. W., Peters, M. L., & Zúñiga, X. (2010). *Readings for diversity and social justice*, (2nd ed.). New York: Routledge.

Allport, G. W. (1954/1979). *The nature of prejudice*. Cambridge, MA: Perseus Books.

American Association of University Women (1992). *How schools shortchange girls: The AAUW report*, Washington, D. C.: Educational Foundation.

Anderson, O. R. (1997). A neurocognitive perspective on current learning theory and science instructional strategies. *Science Education, 81*(1), 67–89.

Andrzejewski, J., Baltodano, M. P., & Symcox, L. (Eds.) (2009). *Social justice, peace and environmental education*. New York: Routledge.

Apple, M. W. (1986). *Teachers and texts*. New York: Routledge.

Archibald, J. (2008). *Indigenous storywork: Educating the heart, mind, body, and spirit*. Vancouver: UBC Press.

Au, W. (Ed.) (2009). *Rethinking multicultural education*. Milwaukee, WI: Rethinking Schools.

Au, W., Bigelow, B., & Karp, S. (Eds.) (2007). *Rethinking our classroom: Vol 1* (2nd ed.). Milwaukee, WI: Rethinking Schools.

Banks, J. A. (2004). Multicultural education: Historical development, dimensions, and practice. In J. A. Banks and C. A. McGee Banks (Eds.), *Handbook of research on multicultural education* (2nd ed.), (pp. 2–29). San Francisco: Jossey-Bass.

Banks, J. A., & McGee Banks, C. A. (Eds.) (2004). *Handbook of research on multicultural education* (2nd ed.). San Francisco: Jossey-Bass.

Banks, J. A., & McGee Banks, C. A. (Eds.) (2010). *Multicultural education: Issues and perspectives* (7th ed.). Boston: Allyn and Bacon.

Banks, J. A., McGee Banks, C. A., Cortés, C., Hahn, C. L., Merryfield, M. M., Moodley, K. A., Murphy-Shigematsu, S., Osler, A., Park, C., & Parker, W. C. (2005). *Democracy and diversity.* Seattle, WA: Center for Multicultural Education, University of Washington. Available at: http://depts.washington.edu/centerme/demdiv.htm.

Bennett, C. (2001). Genres of research in multicultural education. *Review of Educational Research, 71*(2), 171–217.

Biddle, B. J., & Berliner, D. C. (2003). *What research says about unequal funding for schools in America.* Los Alamitos, CA: WestEd.

Bigelow, B. (Ed.) (2004). *Rethinking our classrooms: Vol 2.* Milwaukee, WI: Rethinking Schools.

Bohn, A. P., & Sleeter, C. E. (2001). Will multicultural education survive the standards movement? *Education Digest, 66*(6), 17–24.

Bonilla-Silva, E. (2003). *Racism without racists: Color-blind racism and the persistence of racial inequality in the United States.* Lanham, MD: Rowman & Littlefield.

Bourdieu, P., & Passeron, J. C. (1977). *Reproduction: In education, society and culture.* Beverly Hills, CA: Sage.

Brown, E. R. (2009). Education and the law: Toward conquest or social justice. In W. Ayers, T. Quinn, and D. Stovall (eds.), *Handbook of social justice in education,* (pp. 59–87). New York: Routledge.

Bureau of Labor Statistics (2010). *Employment projections: Education pays. . . . Washington, DC:* U. S. Department of Labor. Available at: http://www.bls.gov/emp/ep_chart_001.htm

Cammarota, J., & Fine, M. (Eds.) (2008). *Revolutionizing education: Youth participatory action research in motion.* New York: Routledge.

Cammarota, J., & Romero, A. (2009). The social justice education project: A critically compassionate intellectualism for Chicana/o students. In W. Ayers, T. Quinn, and D. Stovall (eds.), *Handbook of social justice in education,* (pp. 465–476). New York: Routledge.

Chan-Tiberghien, J. (2004). Towards a 'global educational justice' research paradigm: cognitive justice, decolonizing methodologies, and critical pedagogy. *Societies & Education, 2*(2), 191–213.

Cline, Z., Necochea, J., & Rios, F. (2004). Deconstructing racist propositions: Proposition 227 and the state California. *Latinos in Education, 3*(2), pp. 67–86.

Danielson, C. (2007). *Enhancing professional practice: A framework for teaching* (2nd Ed.). Alexandria, VA: ASCD

Diller, J. V., & Moule, J. (2005). *Cultural competence: A primer for educators.* Belmont, CA: Thompson Wadsworth.

Du Bois, W. E. B. (1935/1995). *Black reconstruction in America, 1860–1880.* New York: Free Press.

Dufour, R., & Eaker, R. (1998). *Professional learning communities at work: Best practices for enhancing student achievement.* Bloomington, IN: Solution Tree.

DuncanAndrade, J. M. R. (2008). *The art of critical pedagogy: Possibilities for moving from theory to practice in urban schools.* New York: Peter Lang.

Edelsky, C. (2006). *With literacy and justice for all.* Mahwah, NJ: Lawrence Erlbaum and Associates.

Edmonds, R. (1979). Effective schools for the urban poor. *Educational Leadership, 37*(1), 15–27.

Eisner, E. (2004). What does it mean to say a school is doing well? In D. Flinders and S. Thornton (Eds.), *The curriculum studies reader,* (3rd ed.) (pp. 297–306). New York: RoutledgeFalmer.

Fernandez, C., Cannon, J., & Chokshi, S. (2003). A US-Japan lesson study collaboration reveals critical lenses for examining practice. *Teaching and Teacher Education, 19,* 171–185.

Flores, J., & Garcia, S. (2009). Latina "testimonios": A reflexive, critical analysis of a "Latina Space" at a predominantly white campus. *Race, Ethnicity, and Education, 12*(2), 155–172.

Fogarty, R. J., & Pete, B. M. (2004). *The adult learner.* Thousand Oaks, CA: Corwin Press.

Fránquiz, M. E., & del Carmen Salazar, M. (2004). The transformative potential of a humanizing pedagogy: Addressing the diverse needs of Chicano/Mexicano students. *High School Journal, 87*(4), 36–53.

Freire, P. (1972/2000). *Pedagogy of the oppressed.* New York: Continuum.

Freire, P. (1998). *Teachers as cultural workers: Letters to those who dare to teach.* Boulder, CO: Westview.

Garcia, S. B., & Guerra, P. L. (2006). Conceptualizing culture in education: Implications for schooling in a culturally diverse society. In J. R. Baldwin, S. L. Faulkner, M. L. Hecht, and S. L. Lindsley (Eds.), *Redefining culture: Perspectives across the disciplines* (pp. 103–116). Mahwah, NJ: LEA.

Gaspar de Alba, A. (1997). *Chicano art inside/outside the master's house.* Austin, TX: University of Texas Press.

Gay, G. (2000). *Culturally responsive teaching: Theory, research, & practice.* New York: Teachers College Press.

Gay, G. (Dec 2003/Jan 2004). The importance of multicultural education. *Educational Leadership, 61*(4), 30–35.

Gewertz, C. (2010). More minorities taking the ACT, but score gaps persist. *Education Week,* August 18, 2010. Available at: http://www.edweek.org/ew/articles/2010/08/18/01act.h30.html?tkn=XMWF4kabeYXvFZGrXwp1H6Ec1dJtQ86SlYHz&cmp=clp-edweek

Gorski, P. (2008a). Peddling poverty for profit: Elements of oppression in Ruby Payne's Framework. *Equity and Excellence in Education, 40*(1), 130–148.

Gorski, P. (2008b). Good intentions are not enough: A decolonizing intercultural education. *Intercultural Education, 19*(6), 515–525.

Gorski, P. (2009). *Social justice and multicultural teacher educators resource survey.* Washington, DC: EdChange. Available at: http://www.edchange.org/survey.html.

Gramsci, A. (1971). *Selections from the prison notebooks of Antonio Gramsci.* New York: International Publishers.

Gruenewald, D. A. (2003). Foundations of place: A multidisciplinary framework for place conscious education. *American Educational Research Journal, 40*(3), 619–654,

Gutmann, A. (1987). *Democratic education.* Princeton: Princeton University Press.

Hains, A. H., Lynch, E. W., & Winton, P. J., (2000). *Moving towards cross-cultural competence in lifelong personnel development: A review of the literature.* Champaign, IL: University of Illinois Early Childhood Research Institute on Culturally and Linguistically Appropriate Services. Available at: http://clas.uiuc.edu/techreport/tech3.html#culture

Hardiman, R., & Jackson, B. W. (1997). Conceptual foundations for social justice courses. In M. Adams, L. A. Bell, and P. Griffin (Eds.), *Teaching for diversity and social justice: A source book* (pp. 16–29). New York: Routledge.

Harris-Britt, A., Valrie, C. R., & Kurtz-Costes, B. (2007). Perceived racial discrimination and self-esteem in African American youth: Racial socialization as a protective factor. *Journal of Research on Adolescence, 17*(4), 669–682.

Harro, B. (2000). *Cycle of socialization.* In M. Adams, W. J. Blumenfeld, C. Castañeda, H. W. Hackman, M. L. Peters, and X. Zúñiga (eds.), *Readings for diversity and social justice,* (pp. 15–20). New York: Routledge.

Hidalgo, N. M., Siu, S. F., & Epstein, J. L. (2004). Research on families, schools, and communities. In J. A. Banks & C. A. McGee Banks (Eds.), *Handbook of research on multicultural education* (2nd ed.) (pp. 631–655. San Francisco: Jossey-Bass.

Hirsch, E. D. (1987). *Cultural literacy: What every American needs to know.* New York: Vintage.

Hlebowitsh, P. (2004). The burdens of the new curricularist. In D. Flinders and S. Thornton (Eds.), *The curriculum studies reader,* (3rd ed.) (pp. 261–270). New York: RoutledgeFalmer.

Holthouse, D. (2009). The year in hate, 2008. *Intelligence Report,* Spring 2009, No. 133. Available at: http://www.splcenter.org/get-informed/intelligence-report/browse-all-issues/2009/spring/the-year-in-hate

Katz, P. A. (2003). Racists or tolerant multiculturalists? How do they begin? *American Psychologist, 58*(11), 897–909.

King, J. E. (1991). Dysconscious racism: Ideology, identity and the miseducation of teachers. *Journal of Negro Education, 60*(2), 133–146.

Kohl, H. R (1994). *"I won't learn from you" and other thoughts on creative maladjustment.* New York: The New Press.

Kornhaber. M. L. (2004). Assessment, standards, and equity. In J. A. Banks & C. A. McGee Banks (Eds.), *Handbook of research on multicultural education* (2nd ed.) (pp. 91–109). San Francisco: Jossey-Bass.

Kozol, J. (1991). *Savage inequalities: Children in America's schools.* New York: HarperCollins.

Kozol, J. (2006). *The shame of the nation: The restoration of apartheid schooling in America.* New York: Crown Publishing Group.

Ladson-Billings, G. (1994). *The dreamkeepers: Successful teachers of African American students.* San Francisco: Jossey-Bass.

Ladson-Billings, G. & Tate, W. E., IV. (1995). Toward a critical race theory of education. *Teachers College Record, 97*(1), 47–68.

Lee, E., Menkart, D., & M. Okazawa-Rey, M. (Eds.) (1998). *Beyond heroes and holidays: A practical guide to K-12 anti-racist, multicultural education and staff development.* Washington, DC: Teaching for Change.

MacGillivray, L., Ardell, A. L., Curwen, M. S., & Palma, J. (2004). Colonized teachers: Examining the implementation of a scripted reading program. *Teaching Education, 15*(2), 131–144.

Marzano, R., J., Pickering, D. J., & Pollock, J. E. (2001). *Classroom instruction that works: Research-based strategies for increasing student achievement.* Upper Saddle River, NJ: Pearson.

May, S., & Sleeter, C. E. (Eds.) (2010). *Critical multiculturalism: Theory and praxis.* New York: Routledge.

McCarthy, C. (1988). Rethinking liberal and radical perspectives on racial inequality in schooling: Making the case for nonsynchrony. *Harvard Educational Review, 58*(3), 265–279.

McIntosh, P. (2004). White privilege: Unpacking the invisible knapsack. In M. Anderson and P. H. Collins (Eds.), *Race, Class and Gender: An Anthology* (pp. 103–08). Belmont, CA: Wadsworth.

Milner, R. (2007). Race, culture, and researcher positionality: Working through dangers seen, unseen, and unforeseen. *Educational Researcher, 36*(7), 388–400.

Minkler, M., & Wallerstein, N. (2003). *Community based participatory research for health.* San Francisco: Jossey-Bass.

Moll, L. C. (1992). Bilingual classroom studies and community analysis: Some recent trends. *Educational Researcher, 21*, 20–24.

Moll L. C., & Gonzalez, N. (2004). Engaging life: A funds-of-knowledge approach to multicultural education. In J. A. Banks & C. A. McGee Banks (Eds.), *Handbook of research on multicultural education* (2nd ed.) (pp. 699–715). San Francisco: Jossey-Bass.

Montecinos, C. (1995). Culture as an ongoing dialog: Implications for multicultural teacher education. In C. E. Sleeter & P. L. McLaren (Eds.), *Multicultural education, critical pedagogy, and the politics of difference* (pp. 291–308). New York: SUNY Press.

Myers, K. A., & Williamson, P. (2002). Race talk: The perpetuation of racism through private discourse. *Race and Society, 4*(1), 3–26.

Nathan, R. (2005). *My freshman year: What a professor learned by becoming a student.* Ithaca, NY: Cornell University Press.

National Center for Education Statistics (2010a). *Participation in education: Language minority school-aged children.* Washington, DC: Author. Available at: http://nces.ed.gov/programs/coe/2010/section1/table-lsm-1.asp

National Center for Education Statistics (2010b). *Contexts of elementary and secondary education: Teachers and staff.* Washington, DC: Author. Available at: http://nces.ed.gov/programs/coe/2010/section4/indicator27.asp

National Center for Education Statistics (2010c). *Digest of education statistics: 2009.* Washington, DC: Author. Available at: http://nces.ed.gov/programs/digest/d09/tables/dt09_008.asp

National Indian Education Association (2005). *Preliminary report on No Child Left Behind in Indian country.* Washington, DC: National Indian Education Association.

National Staff Development Council (2001). *National Staff Development Council's Standards for staff development, revised.* Oxford, OH. Author.

Nieto, S., & Bode, P. (2008). *Affirming diversity: The sociopolitical context of multicultural education* (5th Edition). Boston, MA: Pearson/Allyn & Bacon.

Noddings, N. (2004). The aims of education. In D. Flinders and S. Thornton (Eds.), *The curriculum studies reader,* (3rd ed.) (pp. 331–245). New York: Routledge-Falmer.

Pang, V. O. (2005). *Multicultural education: A caring-centered, reflective approach* (2nd ed.). New York: McGraw-Hill.

Parker, W. C. (2003). *Teaching democracy: Unity and diversity in public life.* New York: Teachers' College Press.

Payne, R. K. (2001). *A framework for understanding poverty.* Highlands, TX: aha! Process, Inc.

Pearson, H. (2010). Complicating intersectionality through the identities of a hard of hearing Koreans adoptee: An autoethnography. *Equity & Excellence in Education,* 43 (3), 341–356.

Powers, A. L. (2004). An evaluation of four place-based education programs. *The Journal of Environmental Education, 35*(40), 17–32.

Pratt, R. H. (1892/1973). *Official Report of the Nineteenth Annual Conference of Charities and Correction* (1892), 46–59. Reprinted in "The Advantages of Mingling Indians with Whites," *Americanizing the American Indians: Writings by the "Friends of the Indian" 1880–1900* (Cambridge, Mass.: Harvard University Press, 1973), 260–271.

Reyhner, J. (2002). American Indians out of school: A review of school-based causes and solutions. *Journal of American Indian Education, 31*(3), 37–56.

Rich, A. C. (1986). *Blood, bread, and poetry: Selected prose 1979–1985.* New York: Norton.

Rios, F. (2009). Home-school-community collaborations in uncertain times. In P. Manyak and M. L. Dantas (Eds.), *Home-school connections in a multicultural society* (pp. 265–277). New York: Routledge.

Rose, M. (1989). *Lives on the boundary.* New York: Penguin.

Rothenberg, P. (Ed.) (2008). *White privilege.* New York: Worth Publishers.

Scheurich, J., & Young, M. (1997). Coloring epistemologies. *Educational Researcher,* 26, 4–16.

Silin, J. (2004). HIV/AIDS education: Toward a collaborative curriculum. In D. Flinders and S. Thornton (Eds.), *The curriculum studies reader,* (2nd ed.) (pp. 229–252). New York: RoutledgeFalmer.

Sinner, A. (2010). Negotiating spaces: The in-betweeness of becoming a teacher. *Asia-Pacific Journal of Teacher Education, 38*(1), 23–37.

Sleeter, C. E., & Grant, C. A. (2009). *Making choices for multicultural education: Five approaches to race, class, and gender* (6th Ed.). Hoboken, NJ: Wiley.

Solórzano, D. G. & Delgado Bernal, D. (2001). Examining transformational resistance through a Critical Race and LatCrit theory framework: Chicana and Chicano students in an urban context. *Urban Education, 36*(3), 308–342.

Spring, J. (2009). *Deculturalization and the struggle for equality.* New York: McGraw-Hill.

Stovall, D., Calderon, A., Carrera, L., & King, S. (2009). Youth, media, and justice: Lessons from the Chicago Doc Your Bloc Project. *Radical Teacher, 86,* 50–58.

Takaki, R. (1993). *A different mirror: A history of multicultural America.* Boston, MA: Little, Brown, & Company.

Téllez, K. (2002). Multicultural education as subtext. *Multicultural Perspectives, 4*(2), 21–25.

U.S. Department of Education, 2003. So many courses, so little time: Engaging middle school students in learning. *Raising the academic achievement of secondary school students (Vol. II of Profiles of Promising Practices).* Available at: http://www2.ed.gov/pubs/Raising/vol2/prof1.html

U. S. Department of Education (n.d.). *Ed Data Express: National snapshot.* Washington, DC: Author. Available at: http://www.eddataexpress.ed.gov/state-report.cfm?state=US

Valenzuela, A. (1999). *Subtractive schooling: U. S. Mexican youth and the politics of caring.* Albany, NY: SUNY Press.

Vaught, S. E., & Castagno, A. E. (2008). "I don't think I'm a racist": Critical Race Theory, teacher attitudes, and structural racism. *Race, Ethnicity, and Education, 11*(2), 95–113.

Vygotsky, L. (1978). *Mind and society.* Cambridge, MA: Harvard University.

Wallin McLaughlin, M. (1976). Implementation as mutual adaptation: Change in classroom organization. *Teachers College Record, 77*(3), 339–351.

Washington, J. (2008). Obama election spurs race threats, crime. *MSNBC,* November 15, 2008. Available at: http://www.msnbc.msn.com/id/27738018/

Waxman, H. C., Padron, Y. N., & Gray, J. P. (2003). *Review of research on educational resilience.* Berkley, CA: Center for Research on Education, Diversity, and Excellence.

Willis, J. (2006). *Research-based strategies that ignite student learning.* Alexandria, VA: ASCD

Yosso, T. (2006). *Critical race counterstories along the Chicana/Chicano educational pipeline.* New York: Routledge.

Zamudio, M., & Rios, F. (2006). From traditional to liberal racism: Living racism in the everyday. *Sociological Perspectives, 49*(4), 483–501.

Zamudio, M., Russell, C., Rios, F., & Bridgeman, J. (2010). *Critical race theory matters: Education and ideology.* New York: Routledge,

Zmuda, A., Kuklis, A., & Kline, E. (2004). *Transforming schools: Creating a culture of continuous improvement.* Alexandria, VA: ASCD.

About the Authors

Francisco Rios, Ph. D., is a Professor in the Educational Studies department at the College of Education at the University of Wyoming (UW). He received his Ph.D. from the University of Wisconsin in learning and instruction after having taught in secondary and technical schools for twelve years. Francisco then worked for ten years at the California State University San Marcos, teaching learning and instruction, multicultural education, and bilingual education. At the UW, he has taught courses in second language acquisition, foundations of education, and multicultural education. He has worked with teachers in-service in California, Wyoming, Wisconsin, Colorado, Washington, and Kentucky.

His research interests include teachers of color, Latinos in education, and preservice teacher education with a multicultural focus. His most recent research has focused on teachers of color in rural, isolated communities. His works have appeared in *Equity and Excellence in Education, Latinos in Education, Teacher Education Quarterly*, and the *Review of Educational Research*. Francisco is the Senior Associate Editor of *Multicultural Perspectives*, the Journal of the National Association for Multicultural Education. He spent spring 2005 as a Fulbright Fellow at the Pontifica Universidad Católica Valparaíso in Chile. Francisco served as program chair for Division K (Teaching and Teacher Education) for the AERA Annual Program, 2007. Francisco serves as the founding director of the University of Wyoming's Social Justice Research Center. In 2008, he received the Distinguished Scholar Mid-Career Award from the Committee of Scholars of Color in Education from the American Educational Research Association.

Christine Rogers Stanton, Ph. D., has over ten years of experience in multicultural education settings, including schools serving Native American communities and urban after school programs for students learning English. She holds two bachelor's degrees in English and Geography from Augustana College in Rock Island, Illinois, as well as a Latin American Studies minor. She obtained her master's in English Education at the University of Iowa, and her Ph.D. in Curriculum and Instruction at the University of Wyoming.

While at the University of Wyoming, Christine also completed a graduate minor in American Indian Studies and a five-course program for effective teachers of Native children. Her scholarly interests, which focus upon community-centered participatory research and Indigenous ways of knowing, were inspired by her work as a language arts teacher and instructional facilitator in a reservation bordertown school. Her works have appeared in *Equity & Excellence in Education* and *Democracy & Education.* Currently, Christine lives in Bozeman, Montana, where she teaches multicultural education and literacy coursework for Montana State University, is learning from communities across Montana, and enjoys adventuring in the outdoors with her husband, Brad.

Index

9 781607 098621